Slovenian
Cookery

SLOVENIAN COOKERY
Second, redesigned edition

Recipes selected by Slavko Adamlje
Introductory chapters on Slovenia by Matjaž Kmecl, PhD
Vineyards and Wines sections by Zdenko Rajher
Translated into English by Rang'ichi Ng'inja and Ian Wraight
Photographs: Janez Pukšič (dishes), Joco Žnidaršič (landscapes), Stane Klemenc,
Matjaž Jež and Peter Skoberne
Editor: Tatjana Žener
Design: Suzana Duhovnik
Layout: Andrej Gale
Published by Mladinska knjiga Založba, d. d., Ljubljana, 2001
Managing director: Milan Matos
General Publishing director: Riko Rižnar
Printed by MA-TISK, d. d., Maribor, 2001

www.emka.si

CIP – Kataložni zapis o publikaciji
Narodna in univerzitetna knjižnica, Ljubljana

641.5(497.4)(083.1)

    SLOVENIAN cookery : over 100 classic dishes / [recipes selected
by Slavko Adamlje ; introductory chapters on Slovenia by Matjaž
Kmecl ; vineyards and wines sections by Zdenko Rajher ; translated
into English by Rang'ichi Ng'inja and Ian Wraight ; photographs
Janez Pukšič ... et al.]. – 2., redesigned ed. – Ljubljana :
Mladinska knjiga, 2001

ISBN 86-11-16136-X
1. Adamlje, Slavko
114484224

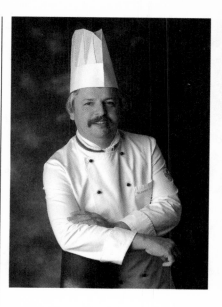

SLAVKO ADAMLJE,

who made the selection of dishes for this cookery book, is considered one of Slovenia's foremost chefs. He is the recipient of several international commendations and awards and has been successfully presenting Slovenian cuisine at various festivals the world over. Slavko Adamlje supplemented his culinary knowledge at the renowned Ritz Escoffier École de Gastronomie Française in Paris. He was also the winner of a gold medal at the 1988 Culinary Olympiad in Frankfurt, a silver medal at the World Championship in Luxembourg, as well as two silver and one bronze medal at the European Championship in Prague. In addition to these, in 1994 he was awarded the Ribbon of Quality by Slovenia's Association of Catering and Tourism.

The publishers wish to express their gratitude to MAXIMARKET – MAXIM RESTAURANT, Ljubljana, where the photographs presented in this book were taken; to DOM d.o.o. for providing the kitchenware on which the dishes are presented, and to SLOVENSKA HIŠA, Radomlje, for the various cottage industry arts and crafts artifacts pictured herein.

Slovenian Cookery

Over 100 Classic Dishes

Založba Mladinska knjiga

Contents

4

Contents

5

Slovenia — a Country of Rich Diversity

It was the contention of the ancient Latins, as well as of contemporary structuralists, that cultivation and, further to this, the preparation and cooking of food is an expression of culture, an example of man circumventing nature. Indeed, we do not consume raw meat, as endowed to us by nature, and can brew a pot of tea, a beverage unknown to nature herself. The same applies to everything that is so punctiliously and conscientiously recorded in cookery books. The food that man prepares, therefore, exemplifies his creativity, singularity and vicissitude. It is known that the Tartars, whilst on their campaigns of pillage and plunder, would soften meat by placing it under their saddles, already a human intervention, a "cultural" act; with the addition of spices this dish has become the delicacy today known as Beef Tartar. Further additives, such as eggs, potatoes, breadcrumbs, cream and the like, as well as the frying of meat has created a variety of dishes far removed from meat in its original, natural form. Each involves the use of fire, a variety of knives and other kitchenware, blenders, the extraction of salt and the conveyance of pepper, the cultivation of crops, and a succession of other procedures. To prepare or consume a meal is to enter an entire, albeit miniature, cultural museum.

It is not our purpose, however, to dwell on such detail. Our intention is merely to point out the fact that cuisine, though it may differ from country to country, is in many ways the result of a miscellany of circumstances — natural, cultural and historical. Wheresoever potatoes thrive, a whole succession of imaginative potato dishes flourish. First, however, potatoes had to be established as a staple, a process which in Slovenia took over a century. In certain German lands, dozens of different

types of asparagus dishes are served when the green is in season, whilst in coastal regions the aroma of seafood fills the air.

Such also holds true for Slovenian cookery, with the added advantage that Slovenia is, historically and regionally, remarkably diverse. Culinary borders within Slovenia roughly follow those dividing the country according to its seven major dialects, namely *Koroška* (southeastern Carinthia), *Primorska* (coastal province, *Notranjska* (Inner Carniola), *Gorenjska* (Upper Carniola), *Dolenjska* (Lower Carniola), *Štajerska* (Lower Styria) and *Prekmurje* (Pannonia east of the Mura river). Indeed, the difference in the vernacular is a consequence of various geographical barriers, the influence of adjacent cultures and division by historical and administrative borders. The classification of culinary regions as found in this cookery book is further justified by other peculiarities, such as the simple fact that the natives of Notranjska, Gorenjska, and Koroška, often had very little in their pantries. At the same time, the larders of Štajerska and Prekmurje have always been more bountiful.

One fact, however, stands for all regions: Slovenes have never been excessively copious in their cookery, possibly with the exception of the Pannonian east. As such, day-to-day cuisine in Slovenia is rather modest, conspicuously marked by the presence of potatoes and cabbage. Lavish feasts were only afforded on special occasions, such as Christmas, Shrovetide and Easter, as well as after the harvest or at weddings. Most of the recipes in this book are of a festive nature — as exemplified by the lavish *Prekmurje Gibanica*; whilst, at the extreme opposite, springtime was marked by indigence, manifesting itself in such extremes as dried and cooked turnip peelings — a renowned dish known as "Hallelujah". Although characteristic, the era of springtime famines has, happily, long gone, and festive cooking is increasingly found on the nation's dining tables.

Vintage Wines of Slovenia

Slovenia is a country of great variety; from the serrated peaks of the Julian Alps in the north, to the rolling hills of Dolenjska and Bela Krajina in the south; from the sunny Adriatic coast and Karst in the West, to the dreamy hills of Slovenske Gorice and Haloze together with their adjacent plains in the east. This land at the juncture of the Mediterranean, the Alpine ranges of Central Europe and the Pannonian Plains, is characterised by diverse climatic conditions, soil and a tradition of viticulture that stretches back two millennia. The first vines on this territory were cultivated by the Celts, a tradition that was later expanded and improved by the Romans, particularly during the reign of Caesar Probus.

Slovenian viticulture has experienced many ebbs and flows, yet we can thank the Slovenian people's love of wine for 21,780 hectares of vineyards which yield some 810 to 930,000 hectolitres of quality wine annually — much to the delight of enthusiasts both at home and abroad.

The quality of wine is dependent on climate, soil structure, grape variety, position of the vineyard and the prudence of the grower. The diversity of Slovenian regions, various varieties and conditions for cultivation have contributed to the availability of a wide range of quality and superior wines, comparable to the most renowned wines of France, Germany and other countries.

Although there have been great advances in the technology of winemaking, the reputation and tradition of a region are still the basic guarantees of quality. Geographic and regional origins are, therefore, most important in the classification of the quality of a wine. On the basis of environmental facts (climate, soil and topography), Slovenia can be divided into three major viticultural

regions: Coastal *(Primorska)*, the Sava Valley *(Posavje)* and the Drava Valley *(Podravje)*. These are subdivided into districts (and sub-districts) which are further divided into cadastres producing characteristic and unique wines. Within each district there are large wineries and cellars which process, bottle and store specific wines of that area. There are also an increasing number of growers cultivating, bottling and marketing their own wines.

Here we must not forget the capital city, Ljubljana, which, due to its long tradition of international wine appraisal, was awarded the commendable title of "City of the Vine and Wine" by the International Bureau for Vines and Wines. Acclaimed judges from the world over appraise wines, which can be sampled by the public each spring at the city's annual International Wine Fair. Slovenian wines have thus been awarded several gold and other medals at this and other fairs. Wine enthusiasts can today purchase excellent wines made from numerous varieties and of different vintages, from the famous cellars in the towns, of Maribor, Sežana and Dobrovo, to mention but three.

Further enhancing this pleasant experience are the so-called "Wine Roads", which traverse the picturesque countryside, as well as a number of wine festivals and exhibitions at which the traditions associated with wine are kept alive. Today there are many aesthetically adorned Slovenian restaurants in which one is able to enjoy an exquisite meal accompanied by excellent Slovenian wines, elevating the whole gastronomic experience to an even higher plane. Whatever your taste in wine, you will probably find something to your liking from a Slovene cellar.

A Harmony of Food and Wine

The custom of drinking wine is a part of the European cultural tradition. Wine is an integral and indispensable part of the menu in vine-growing countries, and the moderate consumption of wine is an expression of esteem and regard for the grower and his harvest. Considering the wide range of wine and food, it is desirable to be versed in the suitable combinations of foods and wines as have been determined over the ages through experience and familiarity with the qualities of wines from various regions.

The selection of dishes, their quality and the purpose of the meal all contribute to the selection of an accompanying wine. In Slovenia a hastily prepared lunch or dinner is taken with only one, carefully selected quality wine which complements a whole range of simple dishes. Such a wine may be of several grape varieties, but originates from the district from which its most important qualities are derived. Thus, specialities in the coastal region of *Primorska* will be served with local wines such as *Kraški Teran* (from the Refosco grape grown on *terra rossa* soil), or blends such as *Vipavec* or *Koprčan*. In the *Dolenjska* region, dishes will be served with the rosé known as *Cviček*, and in *Bela Krajina* with *Metliška Črnina*. The Štajerska region, boasts a broad range of blended white wines — such as *Mariborčan*, *Haložan*, *Ljutomerčan*, *Lendavčan* and *Janževec* — all hailing from different districts. The selection of a wine will be more unconstrained in areas where none is produced. The range of Slovenian wines is so broad that they can be served with almost all local dishes.

Gastronomy today is not as rigid as it once was and allows a more liberal combination of food and wine according to the consumer's taste, though the traditions of individual localities have not been abandoned. The wines recommended for individual dishes are, therefore, merely a guideline and should not be adhered to at all costs. In addition to this, some sense of adventure in seeking new combinations will do no harm. The district and vintage, in addition to variety and colour, are important in determining the quality of the wine.

Taste is usually the decisive factor in choosing a wine to go with a meal; dry and medium-dry wines are more appropriate for the main courses, whilst sweet wines are served with desserts or individually. We might also add that dry sparkling wines and some aromatic white wines make more suitable apéritifs than spirits or other strong drinks. The quality of wine, especially when served during a more festive occasion, should increase gradually, so that *vrhunska* (first quality) wines, characterised by an exalted degree of maturity and special grape-picking methods, as well as *arhivska* (archive) and sweet sparkling wines are served last. A mature and carefully selected spirit also makes a fine epilogue to an elegant dinner. There are, however, certain types of food with which wine should not be taken. It would be very difficult to find a suitable wine for food prepared with vinegar or lemon juice, or for strongly spiced foods. For this reason, salads and certain other hors-d'oeuvres are usually not accompanied by wine. Soups also clash with wine, because both are liquids, and in most cases have incompatible qualities as they are served at very different temperatures. A glass of chilled wine should therefore be taken before the soup or before the second course. Likewise, there is only a very small selection of wines suitable for serving with chocolate desserts; these are primarily highly matured and exceptionally sweet red wines.

A good quality dry *white wine* is the best choice for light hors-d'oeuvres, fish and seafood, unless the dishes are served with strong or spicy sauces. Such wine is also served with poultry, veal, cooked beef and lamb. *Rosés* are comparable to white wines in character and can therefore be served with similar dishes. They are more appropriate for white meat and can be served with stronger side-dishes and hors-d'oeuvres prepared with smoked bacon, paté, pasta or meat. *Cviček* exhibits the character of a rosé. Refreshing and young *red wines* from the Sava Valley, as well as *Kraški Teran*, *Refošk* and *Barbera* from the coastal region of Primorska, go well with ham, pasta with meat, bacon, pork, veal and lamb. Older and more mature red wines, especially from the Primorska region, are excellent with roasted or fried beef and game, as well as strong soft cheeses.

Sweets also play an important role in Slovenian cuisine. They feature several types of layered pie known as *Gibanica*, a cake known as *Potica* and a medley of other desserts. Many of these dishes were once prepared without sugar and, as such, can be served with dry or medium-dry white wines that complement their flavour. More lavish desserts, such as those made with walnuts, almonds, hazelnuts or poppy seeds, demand sweeter wines or wines made from special late-harvest and frost-sweetened grapes. Wine of exceptional quality, from the best vineyards and of the best vintages, especially those aged in renowned Slovenian wine cellars, are served on very special occasions and will help create a truly enchanting atmosphere.

Let us not forget that wine should be served properly chilled and in appropriate wine glasses. Slovenian wines and cuisine deserve our attention and can create unforgettable moments for our guests and ourselves.

Gorenjska
Dishes

Gorenjska

Gorenjska, covering most of Alpine Slovenia, is a beautiful and mountainous region marked by lakes, waterfalls and forests; arable land, however, has had to be etched from the hillsides. With the exception of the central plain around the Sava River, where the soil is relatively fertile, most of the region is very hilly and altitudes can change by as much as 2,500 m within a very short distance. It is a world eminently suitable for tourism, but a curse for farming; rocks can yield little.

In days gone by, the inaccessible parts of Gorenjska served as a refuge for vanquished cultures; echoes of ancient and unusual civilisations in isolated valleys, especially around Lake Bohinj, will not go unnoticed to the discerning eye. The continuous flow of the survivors of vanquished peoples from the plains into these beautiful, but harsh sanctuaries, resulted in an amalgamation of cultures and the evolution of a unique lifestyle and philosophy. To extract a living from the meagre fruits offered by nature, it became essential to apply every ounce of ingenuity and diligence. This resulted in the development of transhumance. Each summer, herdsmen would drive their stock to graze in the high Alpine pastures, whilst fodder for the winter was being prepared in the valleys below. This cultural tradition continues to this day — every spring, herders drive their animals up into the mountains, first to the low-lying pastures, then progressively climbing to higher altitudes, making cheese from the

milk as they go. By mid-September they might reach heights of 2,000 m before retreating from the early advance of winter.

Another source of subsistence proffered by the high Alps was hunting, especially in those isolated nooks where the long arm of the law was unable to enforce the various regulations and prohibitions and where the country teemed with chamois. In the mid-seventies, before their numbers were decimated by blindness and mange, there were as many as 13,000 chamois in the Slovenian Alps; what would once have been considered as a question of survival for the local population, is today deemed an ecological problem. Chamois, however, were not the

only game; red and roe deer in abundance were equally welcome to the hunter. These days, game is still an important source of nourishment for some families.

This difficult mountain life has created a strong bond between man and nature; indeed, he has found it prudent to carefully observe and manage this environment responsibly. It is therefore not surprising that the seeds of modern apiculture were sown in this very place. The people of Gorenjska had long been striving to domesticate the bee, but it was only in the 18th century that a local, Anton Janša, combined experience collected over the centuries with his own ingenuity. It was Janša who took this science to Vi-

enna, from where, under the patronage of Empress Maria Theresa herself, he was to spread it afar. More than three centuries ago, the mores of bee-keeping in Gorenjska were documented by the geographer and polymath, Johannes Weichard Valvasor, who paid special attention to the production of mead. The preparation of this drink was a very complicated and demanding process, which eventually yielded, according to Valvasor, a "very cherished sweet beverage which causes a tantalising sensation on the tongue and whose strength is unmatched by any wine".

One would imagine, therefore, that Gorenjska cuisine is characterised by special and specific aromas and,

indeed, there are a number of dishes that need some getting used to — such as *maslovnik*. This dish is still often made in the traditional manner from old, mellow cream, eggs, etc, and whose taste, aroma and calories make it difficult to eat more that a single spoonful. Rarely can the excellence of this region's cheese, butter, cottage cheese and milk, scented with Alpine herbs and blossoms, be surpassed.

The culinary traditions of the Gorenjska plains have always been somewhat different than the mountains. Carters traversing the ancient routes that passed through the region brought with them elements of international gastronomy. From the Mediterranean came carob pods,

oranges, occasional culinary instructions and even dishes, beverages and habits. Most of these novelties soon disappeared, but some lingered on in their entirety or left their distinctive mark on local cuisine.

Let us finally add that several dishes described within this book, although entered as specialities from the coastal region of Primorska, are in fact Alpine in origin and are frequently prepared in Gorenjska. These include the fairly renowned Trenta Valley *čompe*, which are "nothing but" boiled potatoes with cottage cheese, and the less festive varieties of Idrija *žlikrofi*, dictated by this less than fertile, albeit amazingly beautiful, Alpine and Subalpine world.

Prežganka

("Browned" Soup with Eggs and Chervil)

(see picture, top right)

INGREDIENTS:

100 ml oil

80 g flour

4 eggs

water

a pinch of caraway seeds

salt

chervil (to taste)

Heat the oil in a pan and brown the flour in it, then add water as required to obtain a soup-like consistency. Add salt and caraway seeds and let it simmer for 10 minutes. Beat the eggs and slowly pour them into the soup, stirring all the time. Add chopped chervil to taste and serve immediately.

Croutons can be served with this soup.

Chamois Soup

(see picture, bottom of page)

INGREDIENTS:

1 kg chamois meat

approx. 500 g vegetables (parsley, carrots, celery, cabbage leaves, leek)

black pepper (to taste)

a pinch of nutmeg

a few juniper berries

a spring of rosemary

$^1/_2$ potato

2 fresh tomatoes

or 1 tbsp of tomato purée

salt

Place the meat in a large saucepan of cold water and heat. When it boils, add the vegetables and spices (if using tomato purée, add it last). Salt, reduce the heat and allow to simmer for 2-3 hours, depending on the meat. When the soup is done, add $^1/_2$ a ladle of cold water to clear it. Finally, strain the soup to remove the vegetables. Add *rezanci*, noodles, or other type of pasta, and leave to simmer until cooked.

Šara

(Vegetable Hot-Pot)

(see picture, right)

INGREDIENTS:

1.5 kg potatoes

4 medium-sized turnips

2 turnip-sized yellow kohlrabi

150 g fat

50 g flour

1 tsp sweet paprika

salt

Wash, peel and dice the potatoes, turnips and kohlrabi. Cook the turnips in a separate pot from the potatoes and kohlrabi, and salt both. When the turnips are cooked, drain and place them into the pot with the potatoes and kohlrabi. Prepare a light roux using the fat and flour, then stir it into the vegetables. Finally add the sweet paprika.

18

Wine: Cviček, light rosé or light red wines

Stuffed Potato Dumplings

I N G R E D I E N T S:

Dough

8 medium-sized potatoes

50 g butter

4 eggs

4–5 tbsp of flour

flour, eggs and breadcrumbs for breading, and oil for deep-frying

Stuffing

40 g chopped ham

2 cloves of garlic

a sprig of parsley

white pepper (to taste)

salt

Cook, then peel the potatoes. Chop the ham, garlic and parsley, add salt and pepper and mix thoroughly to make the stuffing.

Mash the peeled potatoes, add the butter, eggs, flour and some salt, and knead it into a dough. Shape medium-sized dumplings, make a hole in each, fill it with the stuffing and close. Roll them in flour, then in the beaten eggs and finally in the breadcrumbs. Deep-fry the dumplings in hot oil. If the oil is too hot, they will remain uncooked inside, whilst if it is not hot enough they fail to turn yellow, absorb too much oil and disintegrate. The best frying temperature is between 170–180 °C.

Wine: Cviček, light rosé or light red wines

19

Žganci

(Cooked Corn Meal)

INGREDIENTS:

500 g maize flour
1 l water
salt
100 g minced lard or pork fat with crackling (for dressing)

Boil the salted water, then add all the flour and cook for 10 minutes. The flour should congeal and form a large ball. After 10 minutes, pierce the centre of this ball with a fork so that its interior also cooks, and allow to boil for a further 15 minutes. Pour off half the water and save it. Stir the flour ball with a fork and break it up into small rather dry pieces — known as *žganci*. Dress with hot fat from minced bacon (*zaseka*) or roasted pork crackling. If the *žganci* are too dry, stir in some of the water in which they were cooked.

Pearl Barley with Prunes

(see picture)

INGREDIENTS:

250 ml pearl barley
2 l milk (or mixture of milk and water)
500 g prunes
salt
100 ml fresh cream

Wash the pearl barley and soak in water overnight. Boil the milk, salt and cook the barley in it. When it is half-cooked, add the prunes. Place on a plate and pour over the cream before serving.

"Usukani" or "Zaroštani" Močnik

(Quick Soup)

INGREDIENTS:

150 g wheat flour
1 egg
1 tbsp of butter or oil
salt
pork crackling, fried onion or milk (for dressing)

Beat the egg. Put the flour into a bowl, then add the egg and mix until small lumps are formed. Work these by hand to form crumbs. Heat the butter and oil in a suitable saucepan. Sift half the crumbs of dough into the hot oil, and mix until they turn yellow and give off a pleasant aroma; add the cold water and salt. When the water boils, add the rest of the crumbs of dough and leave to simmer for a further 15 minutes. The consistency of the mixture must be thick; garnish the soup with pork crackling or fried onion or add some milk.

Gorenjska Dumplings with Cottage Cheese

INGREDIENTS:

Dough

750 g buckwheat flour

500–800 ml water

salt

a little wheat flour

Filling

750 g cottage cheese

2 eggs

250 ml sour cream

3 handfuls of breadcrumbs

salt

pork crackling or breadcrumbs fried in butter (for dressing)

First prepare a dough by mixing the buckwheat and hot water; when it cools, knead it on a wheat flour-covered board. Mash the cottage cheese and mix it with the eggs, add the sour cream, breadcrumbs and a pinch of salt. The filling will be lighter if the yolks are added before the whipped egg-whites, instead of whole eggs.

After letting the dough rest, roll it out to a finger's thickness and cut into small squares. Place half a tablespoon of filling onto each square. Fold the dough over to make small pouches, and pinch the edges to seal in the filling. Boil them in salted water for 10 minutes. When they are cooked, carefully remove them from the water, place in a bowl and sprinkle with pork crackling lard or breadcrumbs fried in butter.

Wine: dry or medium-dry white wines such as Beli Pinot or Chardonnay

Cmoki

(Steamed Leavened Dumplings)

(see picture, below right)

INGREDIENTS:

1 kg flour

30 g yeast

2 egg yolks

0.5 l milk

40 g butter or fat

salt

breadcrumbs fried in butter (for dressing)

Sift the flour into a heated bowl. Break up the yeast and mix it into the lukewarm milk, add the yolks and then whip; also add the salt and molten fat or butter. Pour the mixture onto the flour and knead until the dough no longer sticks to the bowl — an electric mixer can be used for this. Cover the bowl with a cloth and allow to rise for 1 hour. Knead the dough again, make medium-sized dumplings and allow them to rise for a further 15 minutes. In the meantime, heat some water in a broad pan; spread a cloth across the pan and tighten it at the edges.

When the water boils, place the dumplings on the cloth. Cover them with another pan or pot and steam for 15 minutes. When the dumplings are cooked, pierce them with a knitting needle (or similar) to insure they do not sink. Dress the dumplings and serve immediately. Leavened dumplings can be served as a dessert. In this case, add two tablespoons of sugar to the milk and garnish with fried breadcrumbs, cinnamon and sugar. Serve with a fruit compote.

Maslovnik

(see picture, top right)

INGREDIENTS:

500 ml sour cream

500 ml cream

4 tbsp flour

4 eggs

salt

Mix both creams with the flour in a broad pot and heat. Simmer and continue whisking until the mixture becomes thick. When the oil starts to ooze from the mixture, remove it from the cooker and mix in the eggs. Add salt, replace on the heat and stir. Do not allow to boil. Serve hot with black bread or *žganci*.

Wine: Cviček or other light wine from the Sava Valley region

Gorenjska Prata

INGREDIENTS:

2 kg of smoked pig's head or calf's sweetbread
1.5 kg 1-day old white bread
0.5 l milk
fat or oil
1 onion
10 eggs
3 large sprigs of parsley
pepper (to taste)
salt
1 pig's caul or intestines

Wash and boil the smoked pig's head, then allow it to cool; bone it and dice the meat. Cut the bread into cubes and moisten with the milk. Chop the onion and fry it lightly in some fat. Put the bread cubes, meat and onion into a bowl. Beat the eggs and pour over the bread and meat; add chopped pars-ley, salt and pepper and mix it all together. Stuff the mixture into the pig's intestines or caul to form a loaf and place it into a baking tin. Roast slowly until it turns golden-brown. Serve hot as a main course with sal-ad or sauerkraut.

If a less calorific *prata* is required, use lean meat or scalded and diced sweetbread instead of pork.

Wine: a light red wine from the Sava Valley region

Visoko Style Roast Pork

(see picture)

INGREDIENTS:

1.5 kg of pork cutlets

1-2 carrots

6 cloves

6 lemon slices

2 cloves of garlic

a bay leaf

a spring of parsley

pepper (to taste)

1 tsp caraway seeds

salt

fat or oil

Clean and carefully bone the meat. Placing the cutlet on a board with the outer part facing down, make a 1 cm-deep incision along the entire length of the inner (boned) side. Season and sprinkle with caraway seeds. Place a suitable sized carrot, boiled in beef stock, into the incision. Pin the cloves into the meat and line the inner side with thin, halved lemon slices, wafer-thin slices of garlic, the parsley and a

crushed bay leaf. Roll the meat into a roulade, and fasten tightly with a piece of string. Place on a greased baking tray and roast in the oven or, alternatively, grill on a barbecue. Roasting time depends on the size and thickness of the meat. 1 kg of meat takes approximately 1 ¼ hours. Serve with *baked sauerkraut*.

Wine: a red wine from the Sava Valley region

Venison Bohinj Style

INGREDIENTS:

2 kg venison leg or loin
500 g assorted vegetables (for stock)
100 g bacon
50 g fat
peppercorns (to taste)
juniper berries (to taste)
a sprig of rosemary
300 ml sour cream
100 g cranberries
dash of (tarragon) vinegar
salt

Wash the venison and remove any bones. Cut the bacon into strips, dress the venison with the bacon and salt. Fry the remainder of the bacon with the fat in a large saucepan, add the chopped vegetables and spices. Place the venison on top of the vegetables in a baking tin and put into the oven to roast. When the meat browns, baste with sour cream, add the cranberries, some stock or marinade, cover and braise until the meat is tender. Remove from the oven, cut into slices and place on a plate. Add some vinegar to the sauce from the braising and pour it over the venison.

Wine: mature red wines such as Cabernet Sauvignon or Merlot

28

Tržič Prime Rib

(see picture)

INGREDIENTS:

1.5 kg prime rib of lamb

80 g fat or oil

2 onions

3 cloves of garlic

10–12 potatoes

a few juniper berries

pepper

a sprig of savoury

100 ml white wine

salt

Chop the onions and crush the garlic, and then fry in oil together with the juniper berries, pepper and savoury, finally adding some hot water. Scald the ribs in one piece, place them in a pan with the vegetables and add the salt; cover and braise. During braising, turn the ribs several times, add first some hot water or stock and lastly the wine. Peel, wash and halve the potatoes. When the meat has softened considerably, add the potatoes and continue braising. Continue turning the ribs and potatoes during braising.

When both are soft and yellow, remove from the pan, cut the ribs into pieces, place on a plate and garnish with potatoes. Add some water to the stock in which the meat and potatoes were cooked, bring to boil and pour over the ribs. The potatoes can also be cooked separately and added to the ribs at the end, just long enough for them to impart some flavour.

Serve with *štruklji* (see picture — the basic recipe for this very traditional staple can be found on page 59) or a selection of salads.

Wine: dry or mature red wines or rosés

Kranjska
Ohcet

(Carniolan Wedding Feast)

INGREDIENTS:

1.5 kg leg of pork
4 cloves of garlic
salt
a pinch of caraway seeds
50 g fat
2 kg sauerkraut
2 tbsp flour
5 blood sausages (black pudding)
5 grilled sausages
2 tbsp tomato purée

Salt the leg joint. Crush the garlic and caraway seeds and rub them into the meat. Place the meat into a baking tin, pour some molten fat over it and roast.

While the meat is roasting, broil the sauerkraut in a pot with some water. Add the tomato purée and thicken with the flour (mix the flour with some water first). Roast or grill the black pudding and sausages. Finally, pour the fat in which the sausages were roasted onto the sauerkraut. Liver sausage, known as *"jetrnice"* in Slovenia, can be used instead of blood sausages. Place the cooked sauerkraut on a large, pre-heated plate and adorn it with the sliced leg joint and halved sausages atop the sauerkraut. Serve with bread dumplings.

Wine: Cviček or other light rosé

Baked Sauerkraut

(see picture)

INGREDIENTS:

1 kg sauerkraut
50 g bacon
80 g ham
250 ml white wine
2 tbsp minced lard
1 tsp peppercorns
1 tsp juniper berries
1 tsp caraway seeds

Bring the sauerkraut to the boil, strain and dress with 1 tablespoon of hot minced pork fat. Line a shallow baking tin with the bacon, and make a series of 3-cm thick layers of sauerkraut separated by ham, peppercorns and juniper berries. Sprinkle the top with caraway seeds, and pour the white wine and another tablespoon of hot minced fat over the sauerkraut. Place the tin into a preheated oven, and slowly increase the temperature. The dish is done when the sauerkraut turns slightly yellow.

"Netted" Roast Pork

(see picture)

INGREDIENTS:

1 kg boned leg of pork
salt
$^1/_2$ lemon
several sprigs of parsley
a few cloves
a pinch of cinnamon bark
a pinch of caraway seeds
$^1/_2$ tsp pepper
a bay leaf
1 pig's caul, known as a "net"

Rinse and dry the leg joint, then salt and dress it with the garlic and cloves. Cover with lemon slices, parsley sprigs and cinnamon bark, and sprinkle with caraway seeds, peppercorns and the bay leaf. Wrap the meat in the pig's caul, place it in a baking tin and roast. Serve with *stuffed potato dumplings* (see page 19). This dish tastes better if the pork is marinated for a few days.

Wine: red wines from the Sava Valley region, such as Modra Frankinja, Modra Portugalka or Šipon

31

"Hare" Gorenjska Style

(see picture)

INGREDIENTS:

1 pig's caul
750 g minced beef
450 g minced pork
150 g dried smoked bacon
150 ml red wine
1 tbsp chopped capers
2-3 tbsp chopped onion
2 cloves of garlic
1 tbsp chopped parsley
bay leaf
8 juniper berries
a sprig of rosemary
80 g fat or oil
50 g chopped dry bacon
Sauce
1 tbsp flour
1-2 tbsp cranberries
handful of dried mushrooms
crushed herbs and spices

Mix the minced meats; add salt and pepper, as well as the herbs and spices. Knead the mixture thoroughly, place on a board and roll it out. Line with thin strips of dry bacon, roll it into a roulade and wrap it into the thoroughly washed and dried pig's caul. Place into a baking tin, baste with hot oil, and sprinkle with the bacon, chopped onion and diced carrot. Place in the oven and roast for approximately 45 minutes.

When the meat is done, move it to another container and keep warm. Pour off a little of the excess oil and add the flour to the remainder of the fat in the tin. Add the herbs, cranberries and dried mushrooms (soak the mushrooms in some water to re-hydrate and soften them beforehand). Cook the sauce for 30 minutes, strain it and add the wine.

Wine: Barbera, Teran or other full-bodied red wine

Gorenjska Buckwheat Žganci

(see picture at top of page 34)

INGREDIENTS:

600 g buckwheat flour
100 g fat from pork crackling or minced lard
1 l salted boiling water

Pour all the flour into the boiling water and allow a large lump to form; cook for 5-10 minutes, then pierce the mass with a wooden, two-pronged fork so that it cooks all the way through; allow to boil for a further 15 minutes. Pour off half the water and save it. Break up the mass in the pot with a fork and garnish it with hot pork fat or minced lard. If it is too dry, add a little of the water in which the *žganci* was cooked.

Serve with milk.

Krvavice

(Black Pudding)

(see picture, below)

I N G R E D I E N T S:

1 pig's liver
1 pig's lung
½ pig's head
1.5 kg pearl barley
1.5 kg millet
3 onions
1 tsp marjoram
1 tsp freshly ground pepper
1 tsp ground mint
1 tsp basil
salt
approx. 200 g pork crackling
2 l blood
pig's intestines
fat from intestines

Collect the blood during slaughtering, and stir it until it cools to prevent clotting.

Boil the liver and pig's head in the salted water. Boil the lungs separately. When the meat is cooked, pour off the stock and save (it can also be used as a base for soup). When the meat has cooled, mince it or cut it into small pieces.

Clean the pearl barley and parboil it with the millet; allow to cool. Boil the blood. Add the cooled pearl barley and millet to the meat, and add some of the stock if a little dilution appears necessary. Finally, add the blood, herbs, salt, and hot fat and pork crackling. Mix it all together thoroughly. Wash and clean the intestines thoroughly; cut into 15–20 cm lengths, and skewer them at one end. Use a funnel to fill them with the mixture, then close the sausage by skewering the open end. Slowly cook the blood sausages in the stock that remained from the pig's head. The sausages are fully cooked if clear liquid emerges from them when pierced. Remove from the stock, place on a wooden board and let them rest for two or three days. Before eating, roast the sausages in a medium oven, not too hot or the skin will crack.

Wine: rosé or new light red wines from the Sava Valley region

Gorenjska Stomach with Groats

(see picture, bottom left)

I N G R E D I E N T S:

2 kg pork
6 cloves of garlic
200 g millet or buckwheat
40 g salt
½ tsp pepper
water
a pig's large intestine

Mince the meat, squeeze the juice from the garlic and add it together with the salt and pepper to the meat. Mix thoroughly and store in a cool place for a few hours. Sift the groats and knead them into the meat.

Clean the intestine thoroughly and cut it into 30 cm-long pieces. Skewer one end and fill with the mixture of meat and groats (which will later swell!), then skewer the open end. Hang in a smokehouse and smoke as other meat sausages or, alternatively, use immediately — boil slowly for 1 ½ hours until the groats have swollen. Serve cold or hot with sauerkraut or *kisla repa* (grated pickled turnips).

Wine: dry white or rosé wines from the Sava or Drava Valley regions

Kranjske Klobase

(Carniolan Sausages)

(see picture)

I N G R E D I E N T S :

1 part lean pork	
1 part fat pork	
pig's small intestine	
For 1 kg of meat:	
30 g salt	
1 g saltpetre	
1 g ground pepper	
garlic (optional)	
100 ml water	

Mince or chop the meat into small pieces, add the salt, pepper, garlic juice and some saltpetre for colouring. Mix thoroughly and knead for at least one hour. Fill a smooth, small intestine with the mixture. Make into 20-cm long sausages, by twisting in the middle and skewering the open ends. Make sure that the sausages are filled completely; let any air out through piercing, and ensure that there are no air pockets left.

Hang the sausages to dry for a day or two in a cold draft, then smoke for four or five days in cold smoke. Shift the sausages several times during the smoking process. Store in a cool dark larder.

If the sausages are to be eaten raw, add some bacon and use less water. Those that are to be eaten immediately should have 140 ml of water to every 1 kg of meat, and should be smoked for 2 days instead of 4 in order that they retain some moisture.

Wine: Modra Frankinja, the indigenous Žametna Črnina and other dry red wines from the Sava Valley region

Zaseka

(Minced Bacon)

I N G R E D I E N T S :

1 kg fresh bacon joint	
2–3 cloves garlic	
2 bay leaves	
1 tsp peppercorns	
salt (to taste)	
6 tbsp lard	
brine to cover bacon joint	

Refrigerate the bacon, then chop into large pieces, add salt and place in a tub or vat. Add the whole cloves of garlic. Let this mixture stand for 3 days. Cook the bay leaves and peppercorns in brine, cool, remove the leaves and peppercorns, and pour over the bacon. Allow to stand for a few more days. Remove the bacon from the brine, wipe thoroughly and hang until it is completely dry. Smoke the dried bacon in cold smoke for a few days so that it turns a yellowish colour, then hang in cold dry air for 4–5 days. Dice and mince the bacon and add salt to taste. Mix thoroughly, then tightly pack in a tub or similar container. Finally, pour molten lard over the minced bacon. Be careful: if it is not well packed and there are air pockets, it will become rancid. Alternatively, mince the smoked bacon and add crushed garlic. Mix thoroughly and pack well into containers, then pour the lard over it. This dish should be stored in a cool and well ventilated place.

Trout Bohinj Style

INGREDIENTS:

4 kg trout
300 ml oil
100 g strong flour
3 eggs
140 g Bohinj cheese (or Emmental)
100 g breadcrumbs
parsley (to taste)
salt

Remove entrails and clean the trout, cut into several pieces and salt. Beat the eggs, chop the parsley and mix into the eggs; grate the cheese and mix into the breadcrumbs. Roll the pieces of fish in the flour, egg and crumbs, then fry in hot oil.
Serve with roast potatoes, various sauces and salads.

Wine: Sauvignon, Chardonnay, Beli Pinot

Crayfish
Carniola Style

(see picture)

INGREDIENTS:

20 fresh crayfish

2 carrots

a parsley root

20 g celery

$^{1}/_{2}$ onion

bay leaf

caraway seeds (to taste)

150 ml oil

a clove of garlic

a sprig of green parsley

salt

Prepare vegetable stock — cook the parsley root, carrots, celery, onion, bay leaf and caraway in some water. Scrub the live crayfish with a brush, then immediately immerse them in boiling stock and add salt. Let them boil for 10 minutes, then remove, place in a soup bowl and pour some of the stock in which the they were cooked over the crayfish. Dress with chopped garlic and parsley fried in some oil.

Wine: medium-dry white wines from the Drava Valley region

Vodnik Flat Cake

INGREDIENTS:

Dough

400 g strong flour

200 g butter

100 ml water

100 ml sour cream

salt

Filling

5 eggs

100 g sugar

50 g raisins

100 ml milk

350 ml thick sour cream

peel of 1 lemon

60 g flour

80 g walnuts or almonds

Make a dough from the ingredients, knead thoroughly, sprinkle with flour, then cover with a cloth and leave to rest for ½ hour. Knead the dough again and roll it out into a thick layer, place into a shallow earthen dish and bake in a preheated oven.

Mix the egg yolks, sugar, milk, sour cream, chopped lemon peel and flour; finally, add whipped egg whites. When the dough is almost done, pour this mixture over it and put the cake back into the oven to bake. Wash the raisins, crush the walnuts into larger pieces (or peel and halve the almonds) and sprinkle over the filling. Return the cake to the oven and bake until it is done. Sprinkle with sugar and serve hot. In the autumn, forest berries can be used instead of raisins.

Wine: Sivi Pinot, Traminec

41

Shrovetide Doughnuts

(see picture, right)

I N G R E D I E N T S :

1 kg good wheat flour
40 g yeast
3 eggs
100 g butter
6 tbsp sour cream
50 g sugar
salt
approx. 300 ml milk
250 g apricot jam
oil for frying
100 g icing sugar

Sift the flour and put it in a warm place. Crush the yeast, mix it with a teaspoon of sugar and three tablespoons of lukewarm water, then put it in a warm place to rise; when ready, pour into the sifted flour. Whisk the eggs, butter, cream, sugar and salt into a bowl of lukewarm milk, pour into the flour and whisk into a dough. Continue beating for 15 minutes. If the dough is not soft enough, the doughnuts become too heavy — it should be whisked rather than churned. When whisking the dough, make sure not to lift it too much as this will cause holes in the dough which remain in the doughnuts. Continue whisking until the dough no longer sticks to the bowl or the spoon, then cover with a cloth and leave in a warm place to rise.

When the dough has risen, place it on a board, sprinkle with flour and roll it out to one finger's thickness. Use a round pastry cutter to cut discs of dough. Place a teaspoon of apricot jam on a disc of dough; cover with a second disc, pinch the edges together and then trim them with a slightly smaller pastry cutter. The edges of the rings must be well sealed so that the jam does not seep out during frying. The jam must be placed exactly in the centre of the rings, otherwise the doughnuts tend to tip over during frying. Place the doughnuts on a cloth, well spaced from each other, sprinkle with flour, then cover with another cloth and allow to rise again in a warm place. Heat three finger's depth of oil in a deep frying pan. Use one dough-

nut to test the oil. Make sure that the half of the doughnut which has risen more faces upwards and cover the pan. When the bottom half turns yellow, turn the doughnut over. Do not cover the pan again. If all goes well, fry the remaining doughnuts. If the doughnuts rise correctly, they are half-submerged in the oil and there is a pale ring around them. If they rise too little, they are almost entirely submerged and have no pale ring; whilst if they rise too much, they tip over in the oil. If the oil is too hot, the doughnuts brown too quickly, whilst the inside remains uncooked.

To test if the doughnuts are done, pierce them with some implement such as a knitting needle. If the dough sticks to the needle, they are not ready. The doughnuts should not touch the sides, or stick to the bottom of the pan.

When they are done, place the doughnuts on paper or a strainer. Sprinkle with icing sugar whilst still hot.

Wine: Sauvignon, Muškat, Renski Rizling

Brittle Flancati or Drobljanci

(see picture, left)

INGREDIENTS:

1 kg flour

60 g double cream

8 eggs yolks

100 g sugar

2 tbsp lemon juice

2 tbsp rum

6 tbsp white wine

oil for frying

100 g icing sugar

Mix all the ingredients into a dough and allow to rest for a while. Roll out the dough very thinly (the thickness of a knife's edge) and cut into rectangles. Make three or four long incisions in each rectangle, taking care that the edge remains untouched. Interweave the strips and then deep fry in hot oil.

Place the fried *flancati* on a strainer to let the surplus oil run off, then sprinkle with icing sugar.

43

44

Škofjeloški Kruhki

(Škofja Loka Honey Biscuits)

(see picture)

INGREDIENTS:

250 ml honey
450 g rye flour
5-10 potash
1 tbsp cinnamon
1/4 tsp ground cloves
1/4 tsp grated nutmeg
1 lemon (juice and grated peel)
4 tbsp oil

Mix all the ingredients into a dough and knead them thoroughly, place in a greased baking tin and allow to rest for 48 hours. Bake the rolled pastry for 45 minutes; when done, glaze with oil and cut into slices.

Opposite are some examples of these biscuits, as well as the traditional and intricate carved wooden moulds in which they were fashioned prior to baking.

Pumpkin Seed Potica

INGREDIENTS:

Dough
See the Walnut Potica recipe
(page 108)

Filling
400 g husked pumpkin seeds
(or a huskless variety)
50 g sugar
100 g butter or margarine
2 eggs
100 g sugar
10 g vanilla sugar

Prepare the dough; while it is rising, make the filling. Chop the pumpkin seeds, fry them with some sugar and cool promptly (do not grind, as they contain too much oil). Whip the butter, sugar and egg yolks, then add the pumpkin seeds; finally, fold in the whipped egg whites.

Roll out the dough and spread the filling over it, then roll into a roulade-like roll cake. Complete as described in the recipes for other *potica* cakes (see index).

Pumpkin seed *potica* cake has a very unique and pleasant taste.

Dolenjska
and Bela
Krajina
Dishes

Dolenjska and Bela Krajina

Dolenjska is also known to English speakers as *Lower Carniola*, just as Gorenjska is known as Upper Carniola, and Notranjska as Inner Carniola. This part of Slovenia is already far removed from the snow-capped mountains, which can only be seen in the distance on a crisp clear day. Poets, referring to its green rolling hills, describe Dolenjska as gentle. There is little flatland here, what there is being confined to the lower section of the Krka Valley and the Ljubljana Marshes, known as the *Barje*. One would, however, be mistaken to consider Dolenjska as one homogeneous territory, though it would be difficult to draw distinct borders within the region. The district around the towns of Kočevje and Ribnica, for example, has less in common with Bela Krajina and the Krka Valley than does the Gorenjska plain with the Alps! And if the rosé *Cviček* is the epitome of Dolenjska wines, then it should be pointed out that the Bela Krajina wines from the sunny and sheltered slopes of the Gorjanci ridge are starkly different — especially in recent years during which viticulture has rapidly advanced across the region. The Kočevje district, on the other hand, does not have its own wine; it is a forested area, rich in game and renowned for such small specialities as fried dormouse or *dormouse stew*, as well as such large ones as bear.

If it is true, as is claimed by Slovenian ethnologist Vilko Novak, that *štruklji* were invented in Dolenjska, then they represent a truly dazzling trademark of the region. *Dolenjska bean štrukelj*, which also contains cream and eggs, is described in greater detail herein. Nonetheless, the miscellany of *štruklji* and other such dumpling roll-like staples in this land, and in particularly in Dolenjska, is almost limitless; with more than fifty different varieties on offer, this is truly a *"štruklji"* culture. They range from buckwheat with pork crackling, walnuts or tarragon (the first known recipe for which is over 400 years old), to cottage cheese *štruklji* with bilberries. *Štruklji* might incorporate an array of ingredients as diverse as plums, mustard, apples, apple and crackling, potatoes, chestnuts, cured meats, black pudding, poppy seeds, figs, walnuts, chives, even bread and semolina. In addition to buckwheat, maize meal — which can be boiled or baked — is also a common ingredient. Every *štruklji* will invariably contain cream and possibly eggs; the rest depends on the imagination, creativity and inspiration of the cook.

The Dolenjska region once had some formidable islets of poverty, a fact illustrated by a multitude of "recipes", if indeed they can be called that, which have not been included in this book. Many such dishes would perhaps be considered very appropriate by the modern, ecosensitive health food gourmet, yet their frugality was the fruit of necessity: millet porridge which, together with a soup made from a roux-like base and known as *močnik*, was said to "keep Carniola on its

feet"; the hard-boiled millet mush known as *žganci*, and variations on the theme of cabbage can also be said to fall into this category. In spite of its seeming modesty, millet porridge was a ceremonial dish served at weddings. The 17th century polymath and geographer J. W. Valvasor reported that it was served at table shortly before the bride and groom went to bed. The beginning of the wedding ceremony was characterised by the serving of *presnec*, a salty unleavened flat cake — indeed, rather mediocre fare. But here one should consider that in times gone by, local folk went without wheatbread for most of the year; undoubtedly it was considered something of a luxury reserved for festivities. Wheat, if it gave a harvest at all, at

best only returned five-fold on its investment, a much lower yield than that of millet or buckwheat. Bearing this in mind, it becomes easier to understand that porridge and *presnec* were the food of the gentry, and quite suitable for the splendour and significance of the occasion. In Dolenjska, the infertile earth supports only robust varieties of vine and is probably the crux of the reason behind the fact that the gastronomy of Dolenjska is not as lavish as one might expect from a region with such an artistic and jovial character. Krjavelj, a character from a book by the local novelist Josip Jurčič, probably ate meat only once in his life: on the occasion when he and his future wife "liberated", a half-dead piglet from a Croatian

swineherd. In the past, the so-called "Hog Route", a drovers' trail along which pigs were driven from the rich plains of Croatia to the port of Trieste, passed through Dolenjska. Occasionally a pig or two would stray from the herd, or perhaps would be unable to keep up with the pace; the locals were more that willing to help it out of its misery. It was one such occasion that proved to be the undoing of Krjavelj's bachelor status, as well as a blessing for the coming winter.

Not five decades ago, the author Prežihov Voranc wrote that central Dolenjska had some of the most beautiful spots to be found anywhere in Slovenia, but also some of the poorest; where the earth is "a

barren loam, dry and lumpy, despite being dug dozens of times to a depth of a metre". Such an appalling situation is by no means a good foundation for the development of healthy cuisine. Even the gentry of Dolenjska, of whom there were many, rarely indulged themselves beyond the frugal. It would seem that more important matters than what to put on the table preoccupy the minds of Dolenjska folk.

However, let us not lose faith; *Matevž* ("Matthias") with cured pork and sauerkraut, *Easter stomachs* stuffed with buckwheat, and *leg of pork stuffed with sauerkraut*, are all described here, and living proof of good taste and a careful consideration of what one must stock in the larder in order to make life more enjoyable.

The Vineyards and Wines of the Sava Valley Region

The diligent and proud vine-growers of Dolenjska, Bela Krajina and the southern part of the Štajerska region produce pleasant, light red, rosé and white wines with an appetising dry and gentle bouquet. Red wines, from varieties such as *Modra Frankinja* (Blue Franconian), *Žametovka* — an indigenous red vine yielding a wine sometimes known as *"Žametna Črnina"*, *Modra Portug-*

alka (Portugais Noir) and *Modri Pinot* (Blue Burgundy), predominate over the whites of *Laški Rizling* (Italian Riesling), *Chardonnay, Beli Pinot* (Pinot Blanc), *Sauvignon* and *Zeleni Silvanec* (Yellow Silvaner). Dolenjska winemakers are proud of their rosé wine *Cviček*, which is famous for having improved the mood of many a friend. Other pleasant wines from the various district wineries, such as the blended *Bizeljčan* from the Bizeljsko district, *Virštajnčan* from the Virštajn district and *Metliška Črnina* ("Metlika Black"), are also popular. However, this region's sparkling wines are ideal for special occasions, as are the much cherished, naturally sweet wines from the Bizeljsko district.

Dormouse Stew

(see picture)

INGREDIENTS:

4 dormice

100 g butter or oil

50 g flour

500 g potatoes

a sprig of parsley

a sprig of marjoram

peel of 1 lemon

dash of vinegar

black pepper

salt

Clean the meat, cut it into suitable pieces, and fry in oil until it turns golden-yellow. Sprinkle with flour, fry some more and add water. Cut the potatoes into pieces and add to the stew, together with the salt, parsley, marjoram, some peppercorns and the lemon peel. Cover the pot and allow to simmer. When it is done, add a little vinegar and serve.

Wine: from the Sava Valley region, rosé

Chicken Stew with Cviček

INGREDIENTS:

1 chicken

approx. 500 g assorted vegetables for stock (carrot, parsley, celery, leek, cauliflower)

a pinch of marjoram

1 onion

peel of 1 lemon

2 potatoes

80 g oil

50 g flour

20 g breadcrumbs

0.25 l cviček wine

salt

pepper

Clean the chicken, rinse with cold water, put it into a pot and add 3-4 litres of cold water. Bring to the boil, adding the vegetables and salt. Cover and allow to simmer $2 \frac{1}{2} - 3$ hours. Peel and cut the potatoes and add them to the stew when the chicken is almost done; flavour with the lemon peel. Chop the onion, fry it in oil until yellow; make a roux using the flour, oil and breadcrumbs. Add both to the chicken and cook. Finally, add pepper and wine to taste.

Dolenjska Meatballs

(see picture, below)

INGREDIENTS:

1 kg fresh pig's head

600 g pearl barley or rice

300 g millet meal

200 g fat

2 onions

200 ml pig's blood

a pinch of marjoram

pepper

salt

1–2 pig's caul

Clean the pig's head thoroughly, boil it in salted water and then dice the cooked meat. Boil the millet meal and pearl barley or rice, using the water in which the pig's head was cooked. When soft, strain off the grain and add it to the meat. Chop the onions, fry in fat until yellow and add that to the mixture, together with salt, pepper, marjoram and the blood, then thoroughly mix the whole lot together. Shape round lumps — *"kepe"* — and wrap each meatball in some caul before placing onto a baking tray. Pour molten lard over the meatballs and bake in a preheated oven.

Wine: Modra Frankinja, Žametna Črnina (Žametovka), Modra Portugalka from the Sava Valley region

54

Potato Polenta

(see picture, top left)

INGREDIENTS:

1 kg potatoes

70 g butter

2 eggs

250 g flour

100 g grated cheese

100 g fat or oil (for dressing)

salt

Peel the potatoes and boil them in slightly salted water, then strain and add the butter, eggs, flour and half the grated cheese. Knead thoroughly into a potato dough and shape it into an elongated roll; wrap it in a cloth and boil in salted water for 45 minutes. When the roll is done, cut it into slices, dress with hot fat and sprinkle with the remaining grated cheese.

Potato polenta can be served with gravies, grilled or roasted meat, vegetable side dishes, and salads.

55

Bela Krajina Fritters

INGREDIENTS:

Dough

200 ml milk

4 eggs

200 g flour

salt

Filling

1.5 kg fresh pork

a clove of garlic

pepper

salt

500 g fat or oil for deep frying

Beat the egg yolks in milk, add flour, salt, and whisk into a smooth, fluid dough. Whisk the egg whites and carefully fold them into the dough. Mince the meat, add salt, pepper and garlic. Mix thoroughly, then shape into round meatballs, dip each one into the dough and deep fry in hot oil.

Wine: a Bela-Krajina rosé, Metliška Črnina, or a young wine

Bela Krajina Špehovka

(Savoury Rolled Cake with Bacon Filling)

INGREDIENTS:

Prepare the dough following the recipe for the *Walnut Potica* on page 108.

In the meantime, prepare the filling: dice and fry some bacon, then add some beaten eggs; when they congeal, add some chopped parsley, chives or pork crackling. Spread the filling over the rolled dough, then roll into a roulade; place into a baking tin and bake.

Wine: dry or medium-dry white wines from the Sava Valley region

Spit Roasted Lamb

(see picture)

INGREDIENTS:

Clean the lamb, then rub it with salt and allow to stand for some time. Skewer the carcass onto a spit, and brush with oil, fat or butter (which imparts to the meat a better taste). Turn the spit over a charcoal fire until the meat is well done and has turned a golden yellow. Baste continually while roasting. Roast lamb is better if served hot, but can also be served cold with chopped onion or various salads.

Wine: Metliška Črnina

Matevž

(Cured Pork with Mashed Beans)

(see picture)

I N G R E D I E N T S :

700 g dried cured pork
500 g dried kidney beans
500 g potatoes
150 g pork crackling
2 onions
2 cloves garlic
salt
horseradish (to taste)

Boil the meat and cut into slices. Soak the beans overnight, then boil until soft.

Peel, wash, dice and boil the potatoes, then strain them. Add the potatoes to the beans and the water in which they were cooked, and mash together. Dress the mixture with the finely chopped and fried onion and garlic, then add salt. This, the *"Matthi-as"*, should be the same consistency as mashed potatoes. Put it on a plate or in a shallow bowl and dress with the crackling and sliced pork. Sprinkle with grated horseradish or, depending on taste, serve the horseradish separately with a dash of vinegar.

Wine: Cviček

Fižolov Štrukelj

(Dolenjska Bean Roll)

INGREDIENTS:

Dough

500 g flour

2 eggs

2 tbsp oil

dash of lemon juice or vinegar

salt

Filling

300 g dried french beans (seeds)

2 eggs

200 ml thick sour cream

700 ml cream (for topping)

salt

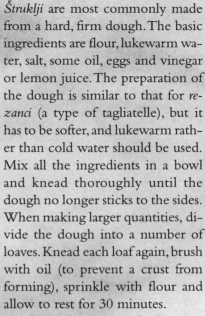

Štruklji are most commonly made from a hard, firm dough. The basic ingredients are flour, lukewarm water, salt, some oil, eggs and vinegar or lemon juice. The preparation of the dough is similar to that for *rezanci* (a type of tagliatelle), but it has to be softer, and lukewarm rather than cold water should be used. Mix all the ingredients in a bowl and knead thoroughly until the dough no longer sticks to the sides. When making larger quantities, divide the dough into a number of loaves. Knead each loaf again, brush with oil (to prevent a crust from forming), sprinkle with flour and allow to rest for 30 minutes.

Cook the beans in salted water, strain, mash and mix with the eggs and sour cream.

Carefully roll out the dough, spread the filling over it and roll tightly into a roulade. Place into a greased baking tin and bake in a preheated oven. Pour the cream over the baked *štrukelj* and allow to stand for a few minutes, before cutting into slices.

Serve as a side dish with meat, pickled grated turnips (*kisla repa*), sauerkraut or various salads.

Wine: dry white or rosé wines from the Sava Valley region

59

Buckwheat Easter Stomachs

(see picture)

I N G R E D I E N T S :

Dough

1 kg flour
30–40 g yeast
400–500 ml lukewarm milk
2 eggs
4 tbsp oil
salt

Filling

250 g buckwheat flour
approx. 1 litre pork meat stock
500 g ham or cured pork
5 eggs
50 g butter or margarine
30 g yeast
approx. 50 g breadcrumbs

Mix the dough ingredients, knead thoroughly and keep in a warm place to rise.

Prepare the filling: cook the buckwheat flour in the pig stock to make a thick creamy soup, adding the eggs, minced ham or dry pork and salt. Allow to cool. Add the activated yeast and enough flour or breadcrumbs for the filling to become spreadable. Keep in a warm place to rise. When the dough rises, roll it out and spread the filling evenly across it. Roll tightly into a roulade, place in a baking tin and pierce several times with a fork. Allow the roll to rise again, and then brush it with whisked egg before baking it in a preheated oven.

Wine: dry red wines from the Sava Valley region, e.g. blends such as Bizeljsko Rdeče, Virštajnčan, or other red wines from Dolenjska or Bela Krajina

Dumplings in Cabbage Leaves

I N G R E D I E N T S :

1 white cabbage
a bunch of chives
120 g minced beef
120 g minced pork
1 onion
1 egg yolk
1 tbsp horseradish
white pepper
salt
50 g butter
50 g peas
200 g peeled tomatoes
approx. 50 ml red wine
100 g cream

Blanch the 8 best cabbage leaves in boiling water and scald the chives. Finely chop half the onion and add it to the meat, then add the egg yolk, salt, pepper and grated horseradish. Shape 8 dumplings from this mixture, wrap them in the cabbage leaves and fasten with the chives. Boil the dumplings in salted water in a covered saucepan for 15 minutes.

In the meantime, fry the remainder of the onions, add salt and pepper, as well as the peas and diced tomatoes to make the sauce. Remove the cooked dumplings from the water, put them into the sauce, add the wine and cream, then simmer prior to serving.

Belokranjska Povitica

(Bela Krajina Rolled Cake)

INGREDIENTS:

Dough

500 g white flour

250 ml lukewarm water

1 egg yolk

½ tsp vinegar

1 tsp oil

salt

Filling

500 g cottage cheese

2 eggs

200 ml thick cream

50 g fat or oil

breadcrumbs (optional)

Make a dough from the flour, water, salt, egg yolks, vinegar and oil, and knead it thoroughly until the mixture no longer sticks to the bowl or the hands. Make two loaves, cover with a warm bowl and allow to rest for 30 minutes.

Prepare the filling: mash the cottage cheese, add the eggs and cream and mix. If the filling is too thin, add a handful of breadcrumbs.

Sprinkle a cloth with flour and roll out two loaves. Brush the dough with oil and roll it out thinly. Spread the filling over half of both of the rolled-out loaves and sprinkle oil over the other halves. Roll them tightly into a single roulade, place into a baking tin and bake in a preheated oven.

Mottled Bread With Carob Filling

(see picture)

INGREDIENTS:

White Dough

1 kg white wheat flour	
20–30 g yeast	
lukewarm water or milk	
salt	

Maize Dough

250 maize flour	
100 g wheat flour	
salt	
30 g yeast	

Filling

500–750 g carob pods	
0.5–1 l milk	
3–5 egg yolks	
200 g butter or margarine	
100 g sugar	
3–5 whisked egg whites	
50–100 g breadcrumbs	
100 ml rum	

First prepare the white dough: mix the yeast with a tablespoon of sugar, two tablespoons of flour and some warm water; keep in a warm place to rise (approx. 10 minutes). Sift the flour into a preheated bowl and add salt. Make a small depression in the middle of the flour and pour the yeast into it. Add as much milk or water as necessary to make a firm dough. Knead it thoroughly, sprinkle with flour, cover with a cloth and keep in a warm place to rise.

In the meantime, prepare the maize dough: mix the maize flour with hot water, make a thick hasty pudding and allow to cool. Then add the wheat flour, risen yeast and salt, and knead — add water only if necessary. Keep in a warm place to rise. Grind the carob pods, cook them in milk and allow to cool. Whisk the butter or margarine with the egg yolks and half the sugar. Beat the egg whites with the remainder of the sugar until hard. Add the butter and yolks, and fold the egg whites and soaked breadcrumbs into the lukewarm carob seeds. Sprinkle some flour onto a board and roll out the white dough to a medium thickness. Put the maize dough onto the white dough and roll it out too. Spread the carob filling over the maize dough, carefully roll into a roulade and place into a greased baking tin. Allow the cake to rise before baking in a preheated oven.

Wine: medium dry or medium sweet white wines such as Laški Rizling, Chardonnay or Sauvignon

Leg of Pork Stuffed with Sauerkraut

(see picture)

INGREDIENTS:

1 small pork leg joint or pork cutlet
1 onion
500 g sauerkraut
sweet paprika (to taste)
bay leaf
pepper
salt
fat or oil

Clean and bone the pork and make a large steak from it. Beat the steak and season with salt and pepper. Cut the sauerkraut into strips. Finely chop the onion and fry in the fat or oil, add the sauerkraut, paprika, one peppercorn and the bay leaf. Cover the pot and braise until the sauerkraut is semi-cooked. Spread the sauerkraut evenly over the steak, roll into a roulade and fasten tightly with string. Put it into a greased baking tin and roast in a preheated oven for approximately one hour. Baste with its own juices throughout roasting.

Wine: mature red wines, e.g. Metliška Črnina, Bizeljčan, or Virštajnčan

Fillet of Pork in Cabbage Leaves

INGREDIENTS:

4 pieces of pork fillet
1 kg sauerkraut
200 g diced bacon
1 onion
1 tbsp sweet paprika
1 tbsp flour
bay leaf
mustard (to taste)
a few ground black peppercorns
salt

Cut the pork fillet into pieces and season with salt and pepper, daub with mustard and fry briefly. Prepare some suitably sized leaves of cabbage: place one piece of fried pork onto each leaf and wrap. Make a layer of cabbage leaves in the bottom of the pot in which the wrapped pork is to be cooked, then place the wrapped meat on the layer of cabbage leaves and sprinkle with the chopped bacon. Add the bay leaf and a few peppercorns, as well as cold water and cook on a moderate heat for approximately one hour. Make a roux from the oil in which the meat was fried, using the sweet paprika and flour; add it to the meat. Cook for a further 30 minutes before serving.

Wine: mature red wines, e.g. Metliška Črnina, Bizeljčan or Virštajnčan

Koroška
Dishes

Koroška

Today, only a small corner of Carinthia, called *Koroška* by the Slovenes, remains inside what is now the Republic of Slovenia. However, little more than a millennium ago this large region formed the core of the Slovenian nation. Indeed, in its time Carinthia was an independent duchy, known as "Greater Carantania", which stretched as far south as the Gulf of Rijeka. The nucleus of this state was the Krn Castle (Karnburg), some 8 km north of the city of Klagenfurt in Austria. During the early 8th century, a new class of Slav yeomen emerged who elected their ducal rulers. The ancient ritual surrounding the enthronement of the Carinthian Dukes and its democratic nature are believed to have inspired Thomas Jefferson to incorporate some of its basic element into the constitution of the United States. Of primary influence was the symbolic delegation of power from the people to the incumbent, on which occasion the formal contract of citizenship was ritually and solemnly renewed: "We give you the power, you give us protection and rights, and together we shall work towards achieving common prosperity". The last such historical coronation took place as late as 1414, by which time Carinthia had been incorporated into the Frankish, and later the German, empires. Nevertheless, despite the succeeding centuries of Germanic hegemony, its impact continued in various forms.

Perhaps it is somewhat unusual that all this should be mentioned in a cookery book; furthermore, when considering the history of this land, one might expect the cuisine of Koroška to be fit for nobility, royalty even. This, however, is not the case. It would seem that the Carinthians used up most of their talent on music, leaving little for the kitchen. Indeed, the people of this land have an exceptional ear for music; their dishes, on the other hand, are ascetic, mellow and lyrical, much like the people themselves. They strive to create modest culinary poetry from poverty, and a grand dish from a rather mediocre piece of meat. Their menus veritably sing: *močnik, "žganki" (žganci)*, varieties of fruit *žlikrofi*, as well as a whole range of potato and buckwheat dishes featuring just about anything that will grow in their mountain valleys. Easter, and other festive occasions, are opportunities to serve a dish known as *"šarkelj"* or *"šartelj"* and for children to exchange Easter *"pisanice"* or Easter eggs. Such "eggs" were certainly never of chocolate and weren't necessarily, as is the custom in other parts of Slovenia, ordinary painted hardboiled eggs; they could also be in the form of unleavened bread cakes inside which some coins were hidden. Such cakes could be large or small, and yellow in colour — signifying the use of a large amount of eggs and butter, or pale and lightly baked — masking its lack of luxury.

Honey features heavily in the cuisine of Koroška; the people believe

that it increases strength and virility. A quick glance at any menu will also reveal that their average meal contains more vegetables than any other in Slovenia. Dry sausages from Koroška are among the nation's hardest; as the most thoroughly cured, they are also among the healthiest and tastiest, and as such, represent an enviable culinary achievement. As in all mountainous areas, life here is hard and laborious, and care must be taken to prevent any produce from spoiling. The overriding principle concerning preserving meat is, therefore, "that it is better to cure too much than too little", something for which the climatic conditions are eminently suited.

Local variations of typical Sloveni-an dishes are, of course, also to be found in Koroška. Those that differ are in the most part recent acquisitions rather than expressions of local custom and tradition. The blame for this, according to the Slovenian poet Valentin Vodnik's preface to his cookbooks of 1799, the first of their kind in the Slovene language, falls on the men:

"Male cooks — in contrast to their diligent, clean and fair female counterparts — believe that they are more clever and try to outwit the womenfolk; and what has been the consequence of this? They have, indeed, invented all sorts of dishes, but dishes harmful to one's health. They have introduced a whole variety of unhealthy foods hidden behind a cloak of fancy names."

To state that good cooking is the result of man's wit and craft would, of course, be an over-simplification of the matter. There were always those who, when enjoying a savoury but otherwise unknown dish, asked what was in it and how to prepare it. But since this area has always been something of a crossroads of Europe, it is self-evident that a variety of new dishes found its way here and was readily adopted by the locals; from Austrian *wiener schnitzels* to Turkish and Serbian *čevapčiči*, from Italian macaroni to Hungarian goulash.

This book, however, presents only the "cream" of old, authentic Slovenian dishes, including those from Koroška.

Koroška
Cream Soup

I N G R E D I E N T S:

1 kg pig's trotters
approx. 500 g vegetables to make stock
0.5 l sour cream
50 g flour
1–2 egg yolks
salt

Clean the trotters and vegetables. Boil some water in a pot, add salt and cook the trotters and vegetables until the meat is svitably tender. Remove the trotters from the pot, bone the meat and chop it into small pieces. Strain off the stock, then put it back on the heat. When it comes to the boil, whisk in the mixture of flour and sour cream, then thicken the soup with one or two egg yolks.

Add the pieces of meat and serve.

70

Mavžlji

(Meatballs)

(see picture)

INGREDIENTS:

1 kg pig's head including the brains
150 g white bread
50 g butter
1 small onion
4 tbsp milk or cream
200 g rice
a clove of garlic
3 sprigs of parsley
a little pimento
peel of 1 lemon
a little marjoram
1 pig's caul

Wash the pig's head, remove the brains and wash them. Cook, the head in water and save the stock. Boil the brains separately, or fry them in some fat. Remove the cooked meat from the skull and chop it into small pieces; similarly chop the boiled or fried brains.

Soak the bread in water, then squeeze it. Chop the onions and parsley and crush the garlic. Fry the onion in some butter and add the parsley, garlic and bread. Stir fry for a few minutes, then add the milk; stir well, add the spices and allow to cool. Afterwards, season with the pimento, lemon peel and marjoram and add the brawn.

Cook the rice in the stock from the pig's head — it must be "al dente" — allow it to cool, then add it to the meat filling and salt. If the filling is too dry, stir in some stock. Thoroughly wash the pig's caul and spread it over a table. Using a tablespoon, scoop the filling onto the caul, making sure that the tablespoons of filling are sufficiently distant from each other. Using a knife, cut the caul around the scoops of filling and wrap them in it to form the meatball-like *mavžlji*. Place them in a special tray (see picture) or tin and bake in the oven.

This dish can be served hot or cold. Serve hot with sauerkraut, pickled grated turnip (*kisla repa*) or a salad.

Wine: a rosé, a light red or a young dry red wine

Ubrnenik

(see picture)

INGREDIENTS:

400 g strong wheat, maize or
buckwheat flour

fat or oil for frying

250 ml cream

400 ml milk

salt

Fry the flour in a large saucepan.
Boil the milk and cream in a separate pan, salt, then pour it over the
flour and stir rapidly. Shape small
balls from the mixture. Serve with
white coffee, milk or sour milk. It
can also be eaten cold.
Ubrnenik made with sour cream and
cottage cheese has a slightly sour
taste.

Masovnik

INGREDIENTS FOR 1 PERSON:

1 tbsp butter	
1 tbsp wheat flour	
100 ml milk	
a pinch of salt	

Fry the flour in butter until it turns yellow, then add the hot salted milk. Stir until the mixture no longer sticks to the bottom and sides of the pan. Serve hot with coffee or tea.

Žganci with Honey

INGREDIENTS:

3 l brine	
800 g flour (strong wheat, maize or buckwheat flour)	
8 tbsp honey	
4 tbsp fat	

Boil the brine and pour in the sifted flour. The water must not boil too vigorously, or the flour will not remain in a neat lump as required. Allow to boil for 15 minutes, then turn the lump over, pierce with a fork and cook for a further 10 minutes. Pour off approximately 1.5 l of the water. Heat the fat, pour it into the mass and stir. Crumble the *žganci* into a bowl, and pour over the warm honey prior to serving.

Buckwheat Vzhajanci

(see picture)

INGREDIENTS:

250 g white (wheat) flour

500 g buckwheat flour

40 g yeast

lukewarm water

salt

pork crackling (for garnish)

Mix the yeast with some lukewarm water and a teaspoon of flour. Put in warm place and allow to rise. Make a dough from both sorts of flour, yeast, water and salt; knead thoroughly and allow to rise. When the dough has risen, sprinkle some white flour over a board, place the dough on it, knead and then make into one large or several smaller loaves. Boil this/these in salted water. When done, remove carefully from the water, cut into slices and garnish with the pork crackling.

Vzhajanci are served as a side dish with meat, sauerkraut, grated pickled turnip (*kisla repa*) or other vegetables; or, alternatively, as an individual meal with salad.

74

Fruit Žlikrofi

INGREDIENTS:

Dough
500 g flour

3 eggs

2 tbsp oil

water

Filling
750 g of one or several types of dried fruit — prunes, pears, apples

100 g butter

100 g breadcrumbs

100 g sugar

1 tsp cinnamon (depending on taste)

milk or cream

Dressing
100 g fat, oil or butter

50 g breadcrumbs

Make a dough from the flour, eggs, oil and water. The dough should be somewhat softer than that used for *rezanci*. Knead thoroughly, sprinkle the dough loaf with flour, cover with a cloth and allow to rest for at least 30 minutes.

In the meantime, prepare the filling: grind the dried fruit, fry the breadcrumbs in some butter and add them to the fruit; season with cinnamon and sugar. Stir thoroughly, and if it is too dry, add some milk or cream.

Roll the dough out thinly and cut into rectangles. Place a walnut-sized lump of filling onto each rectangle. Fold the dough over the filling. Brush the edges with egg white and pinch them together to keep the filling inside, then trim the edges with a pastry trimmer. Cook the *žlikrofi* in salted water for 10-15 minutes, strain thoroughly. Dress with breadcrumbs fried in the oil, fat or butter.

Serve with a compote or a fruit salad.

Koroška Stuffed Rezanci

(see picture)

INGREDIENTS:

Dough

500 g flour
3 eggs
2 tbsp oil
a little milk
salt
breadcrumbs fried in butter or oil (for dressing)
ingredients for the **Filling** (see below)

Make a dough from the flour, eggs, salt, oil (and milk if necessary). Knead thoroughly, sprinkle with flour, cover with a cloth and allow to rest. When the dough has rested, knead it again and fashion into an oblong loaf which should then be cut into finger-thick slices. Roll out only half of each slice, place some filling (see below) on it, cover with the rolled part of the dough and then again with the unrolled part — so that the filling is covered twice. Pinch the edges together to seal and place each *rezanec* gently into boiling water to simmer for 15 minutes. When the *rezanci* are done, remove from the water, place in a bowl and pour the dressing over them. The dressing depends on the filling. Sweet *rezanci* should be dressed with breadcrumbs fried in butter or oil; savoury *rezanci* should be dressed with pork crackling, minced lard or fried breadcrumbs.

Cherry Filling
Mix together ground dried cherries or morello cherries, sugar, cinnamon, breadcrumbs and one or two eggs. Add enough double cream to obtain a suitably thick mixture.

Cottage Cheese Filling
Fry some breadcrumbs in butter, add mashed cottage cheese, chopped parsley, one or two eggs, butter, salt and thick sour cream. Stir thoroughly.

Apple or Pear Filling
Grate the apples or pears, add breadcrumbs fried in butter, sugar and cinnamon powder. Ground walnuts or poppy seeds can be added according to taste.

Fresh Pork Filling
Cook a fatty piece of pork and allow to cool. Chop or mince the meat; add two eggs, breadcrumbs, two tablespoons of cream, chopped parsley, pepper and crushed garlic.

Wine: a Slovenian medium dry or medium sweet white wine

Koroška Šarkelj

(Leavened Sponge Cake)

INGREDIENTS:

Dough

500 g flour

100 g butter

3 egg yolks

200–300 ml milk

30 g yeast

100 g sugar

salt

Filling

200 g raisins

2 tsp cinnamon powder

100 g sugar

Prepare the yeast: mix it with two teaspoons of flour, 1 teaspoon of sugar and 50 ml milk. Put in a warm place to rise.

Stir the butter with the sugar and egg yolks until smooth. Add flour, milk and salt, then mix; finally, add the yeast. Knead thoroughly for 10 minutes and allow to rise. Put the dough on a board sprinkled with flour, and roll out to a thickness of 1 cm. Sprinkle the dough with the raisins, cinnamon and sugar, roll it into a roulade and place in a special *šarkelj* baking tin. Allow the dough to rise again in the tin. Baste with whisked eggs (including the whites) and bake in a medium hot oven.

Wine: medium sweet white wines from the Drava Valley region

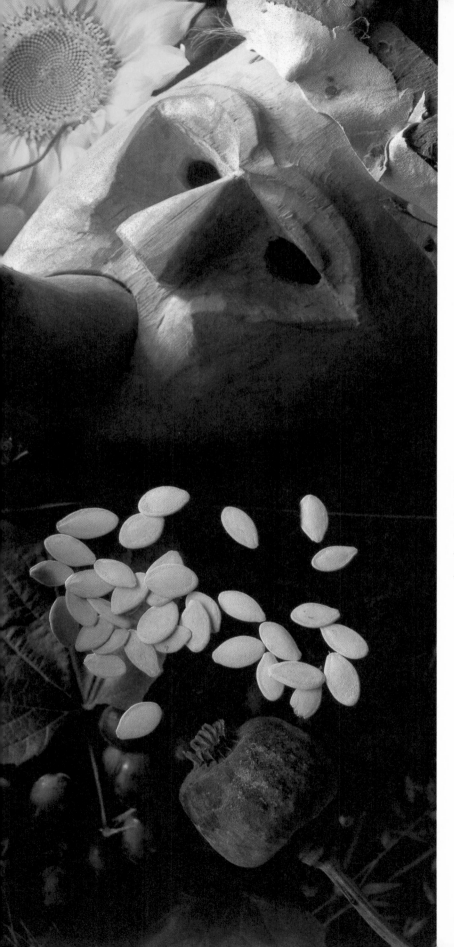

Štajerska and Prekmurje Dishes

Štajerska and Prekmurje

These, the lands of eastern Slovenia, have always been relatively prosperous. There are, of course, also some significant differences between areas, such as between the Savinja Valley, which has been described as the "Promised Land", and the poor Kozjansko district; or between the Drava Plain and the Haloze Hills, or even between the lowlands of Ravensko and hilly Goričko in the far northeast of the country. Gastronomic diversity is also quite evident, even in such details as the differences between the fillings of the pie-like *gibanica*s which emanate from the Prekmurje region in comparison with those from Prlekija or Haloze. One is a lavish dessert, containing walnuts, poppy seeds, cream, cottage cheese, fruit and honey, whilst the other is a thin, cottage cheese and sour cream "pizza" which betrays a humble way of life. In general, however, the regions of Štajerska and Prekmurje are considered to comprise some of the most outgoing, jovial and culinarily opulent parts of Slovenia.

A neat distinction also exists between Štajerska and Prekmurje from a purely geographical perspective. Prekmurje extends along the left bank of the Mura river in the extreme northeast of the country. The broad and meandering Mura was once a disputed border between the German and Hungarian kingdoms, a fact which led to much pillaging and destruction of these parts by the opposing armies. Once it was finally agreed that the Mura river should become the frontier be-

tween these two states, affluence returned to this corner of the Pannonian Plain, as is witnessed by the magnificent 14th century churches in Martjanci, Turnišče, Selo and Murska Sobota. By way of this border, Prekmurje was separated both politically and culturally from Štajerska and the rest of Slovenia — and remained so until the end of the First World War. This separation facilitated independent and unique development, the elementary culture of which was influenced by the melancholy of the antique. Here ethnologists speak of "white Slovenia" in reference to the endemic coarse linen bleached in the sun which, until fairly recently, was spun, woven and worn by the people of Prekmurje (as well as Bela Krajina), and to the habit of local people whitewashing their small earth-and-straw homes on festive occasions. Indeed it is in Prekmurje that the earliest semblances of Slovenian culture have persisted — through the early Medieval duchies ruled over by Kocelj and Pribina and possibly as a result of ancient ethnic links with the Slavs of Moravia and Slovakia. Elements of this culture have been preserved to this day. At the same time, the Hungarian language has borrowed over one thousand words from the Slovenes and Slovaks and, in return, the Hungarian art of good cooking has been borrowed by this Slovenian border region. A good *bograč* for example, which, with all the many kinds of meat and other delicacies it contains, can only be afforded in a prosperous place. Finally, as unusual as

it may sound, there are profound differences between the Protestant and Catholic cuisines in this region. Whereas Protestants could have the number of offspring they willed, Catholics had as many as God enabled: Protestant farmsteads were, therefore, larger, wealthier and not as fragmented as those belonging to Catholic families, a state of affairs that clearly had its effects at the dining table. Common to all of eastern Slovenia, however, is occasional culinary immodesty — primarily at weddings, but also during other festive occasions. It is a rule at such events that good food "must never run out" — even if the celebration continues into the third or fourth day. In fact, these are opportunities to exhibit the best of Štajerska and

Prekmurje cuisine. It is not just the serving of mountains of pastries and breads, but also an extravagance of every conceivable delicacy, from a variety of meats preserved in *tunjka* and wedding *štruklji,* though variations of the cake known as *potica* to the almost obligatory *sour soup.* Indeed, this soup, once considered to be of medicinal value especially when nursing a hangover, played a similar role to coffee. This impressive imagination of the people of Štajerska and Prekmurje is at its most expressive during *"koline"* — the traditional feast that surrounds the slaughtering of a pig. Their familiarity and knowledge of charcuterie extends not only to classical sausages and salamis, but to at least a dozen special varieties of the same, along with cheese, milk, sour milk and pearl barley stocks, to mention but a few. Some of these dishes are served only during *koline.* Here we might mention *godlja,* which can be anything from the water in which blood sausages (in Slovenia known as *krvavice*) have been cooked and in which one or two have burst and their contents spilled, to a dish prepared according to a special recipe.

Another very common ingredient in the cuisine of Štajerska and Prekmurje is pumpkin seed oil. This salad dressing might be somewhat unpalatable and difficult to digest for a Slovene from the west of the country, just as the olive oil commonly used in the coastal region of Primorska might not be too much to the liking of the easterner. Nonetheless, any connoisseur will confirm that a radish-and-bean salad dressed with pumpkin seed oil, for example, or a cabbage, cucumber or even a lettuce salad crowned with the same, is a true delicacy indeed. And whilst on the subject of salads, in those areas of Štajerska where hops are grown, especially in the Savinja Valley, a salad is prepared from cooked *hop sprouts*; those who have tried it admit that they have tasted worse.

The common denominator for the cuisine of Štajerska and Prekmurje is, therefore, luxury and a panoramic abundance of dishes; from the modest to the outright lavish, with or without meat, simple or flagrantly complicated.

The Vineyards and Wines of the Drava Valley Region

This is Slovenia's largest wine region, although it comes in second to the coastal region of Primorska in terms of the quantity produced. It encompasses north-eastern Slovenia and includes the vineyards around the Pohorje Massif and Kozjak Hills near Maribor, as well as the hills of the Slovenske Gorice, Haloze, Prekmurske Gorice and Goričko. Retired Roman legion-

naires, who established the town of Poetovio (Ptuj) in 69 AD, had already savoured wine from the Haloze Hills. Viticulture suffered a great blow with the collapse of the Roman Empire; it was not until centuries later that monks from this region's monasteries revived the culture and contributed to its steady development. Wine-making has a very long tradition here and the region boasts several renowned cellars.

The distinguishing characteristic of this region are its fine white wines, almost all are invariably quality *(kakovostno)* and superior quality *(vrhunsko)*, especially the single variety (unblended) wines. Of exceptional fame are the wines from spe-

cially matured and selected grapes — such as "late vintage" *(pozna trgatev)*, "selected grape" *(jagodni izbor)*, "dry grape selection" *(suhi jagodni izbor)*, as well as "iced wine" *(ledeno vino)* made from frosted grapes. The traditional varieties of grape, such as *Laški Rizling* (Italian Riesling) and *Šipon* (Mosel-Furmint) are considered important. Other varieties such as *Chardonnay, Beli Pinot* (Pinot Blanc), *Sivi Pinot* (Pinot Gris-Rulander), *Renski Rizling* (Rhine Riesling), *Sauvignon, Zeleni Silvanec* (Yellow Silvaner), *Traminec* (Traminer) and *Rumeni Muškat* (Yellow Muscatel) are also grown. Wines from the central and eastern Štajerska districts as well as Prekmurje have an excellent bou-

quet, good aroma, pleasant acidity and an appealing greenish-yellow colour; they are similar to the renowned wines of the Rhinelands. The warm and dry Pannonian climate guarantees very good quality dry and medium dry table wines, as well as exceptional superior quality sweet wines which represent the cream of Slovenian viticulture.

Štajerska Sour Soup

(see picture, top)

I N G R E D I E N T S :

500 g fresh lean pork
1 pig's heart
1 pig's tail
1 onion
carrots
parsley
celery
marjoram
bay leaf
peppercorns
salt
4 cloves garlic
50 g flour
500 g potatoes
3 tbsp sour cream
2 tbsp vinegar

Cut the meat and the vegetables for stock into pieces and boil in 1.5 to 2 litres of salted water together with the herbs. Cut the potatoes into pieces and add them to the soup stock after the meat has softened somewhat. Mix in the cream and flour to thicken, and continue to cook until all the ingredients are soft. Finally, add some vinegar. The meat can also be boiled in one piece. When it is cooked, cut it into pieces and add to the soup only when the vegetables and potatoes are done. The rest of the procedure remains the same.

Wine: dry white wines from Štajerska

Potato Soup With Milk

(see picture, below)

INGREDIENTS:

1.5 kg potatoes
1 l milk
80 g butter or margarine
1 carrot
1 onion
a stick of celery
a sprig of parsley

Wash the vegetables, peel the potatoes and boil them all in salted water. When cooked, mash or blend
them into a smooth purée and add
boiling milk. Finally, add molten
butter or margarine and serve.
If solid vegetables are preferred, dice
them instead of puréeing, and do
not strain the soup.

85

Štajerska Bržole

(Styrian Prime Rib)

INGREDIENTS:

8 prime ribs of beef
80 g fat or oil
1 large onion
100 g butter
1 tbsp sardine paste
200 ml stock or water
salt

The cut should be from a young animal. Mix the sardine paste with the butter and keep the mixture in a cool place. Remove excess fat from the rib steaks, make a few incisions into each to avoid bowing; beat, then lightly salt. Grate the onion and squeeze the juice over one side of the ribs. Fry the meat lightly on both sides and place into a different pan one on top of another, spreading the sardine butter between layers. When all the steaks are done, cover the pan and allow to stand in a warm place for about 10 minutes. Pour the stock or water into the pan in which the steaks were fried and bring to the boil, then strain the gravy. Serve the *bržole* on a plate and pour the gravy over them. Serve with *rezanci*, noodles, dumplings, *žganci* or white polenta.

Wine: Modra Frankinja or other red wine from Štajerska

Bograč

(see picture)

INGREDIENTS:

400 g beef
400 g fresh pork
1 kg potatoes
100 g bacon
500 g onions
1 tsp sweet paprika
2 cloves of garlic
a pinch of caraway seeds
a bay leaf
1 tbsp tomato purée
salt

Cut the meat and bacon into pieces and finely chop the onions. Heat the bacon in oil, and fry it together with the onions. Add the paprika and remaining meat, followed by enough water to braise. Braise gently for approximately 1 hour.

In the meantime, peel the potatoes, cut into pieces and add to the meat. Season with the spices and salt and cook for a further 30 minutes in a covered saucepan. In the Prekmurje region, *bograč* is prepared in a special earthen pot.

Wine: Šipon, Laški Rizling, or other dry white Štajerska or Prekmurje wine

Turkey with Mlinci

(see picture)

INGREDIENTS:

Turkey

1 young turkey	
150 g fat or oil	
stock or water for basting	
salt	

Stuffing

1 kg cooked sweet chestnuts	
250 g fresh sausages	
100 g spring onions	
3 cloves garlic	
1 tbsp brandy	
salt, pepper	
butter, oil	

Mlinci

600 g white flour	
200 ml lukewarm water	
1 egg	
salt	

Cut the turkey liver into thin slices. Cut the sausages and fry them thoroughly in butter together with the onion and garlic; add the liver and fry some more. Peel the cooked chestnuts, purée them and add to the liver. Season with salt, pepper and the brandy. Mix thoroughly, then stuff the turkey, carefully stitching closed the opening. Put the turkey onto a baking tray, pour some hot fat over it and roast in an oven for approximately 3 hours. Baste it several times during roasting.
In the meantime, prepare the *mlinci*

(flat cakes); make a dough from the flour, water, salt and egg. Cut it into several small loaves, knead each one thoroughly and allow to rest for 30 minutes. Roll them out flat, then bake. When the turkey is almost done, break up the *mlinci*, pour boiling water or milk over them and allow to stand for a while. Strain the liquid from the *mlinci*, then place them on the baking tray around the turkey; continue roasting until they are done.

Arrange the finished *mlinci* on a large plate or in a shallow dish, carve the turkey and place the pieces of turkey on them. Serve with salad.

Wine: white or light red wines from Štajerska, e.g. Modri Pinot or Laški Rizling, Šipon, Chardonnay

Dressed Hop Sprouts

I N G R E D I E N T S:
a bunch of young fresh hops sprouts
breadcrumbs
butter

The hops sprouts must still be soft; clean and rasp them in a similar way to asparagus. Cook the hops in salted water, and fry the breadcrumbs in butter. When the hops are cooked, strain and dress them with the fried crumbs.

Hop Salad

(see picture, bottom right)

INGREDIENTS:

a bunch of young fresh hops sprouts

50 ml oil

100 ml vinegar

salt

The hops must be picked very young, when still red. Boil them in salted water. When they soften, strain, put in a bowl and dress with vinegar and oil.

Mežerli

(see picture, left)

INGREDIENTS:

1–1.5 kg veal or pig's lung
(with part of the heart)

3 tbsp of fat or pork crackling

2 medium-sized onions

500–750 g stale white bread

1–2 eggs

250 ml milk

100 ml sour cream

a pinch of marjoram

pepper, salt

fat for greasing the baking tray

Wash the lungs, boil in salted water and allow to cool. Save some of the water in which they were cooked. Once the lungs have cooled, remove the gullet and mince them. Chop the onions finely, fry in fat until yellow and add to the lungs. Season with marjoram and pepper. Cut the bread into small cubes, pour the beaten eggs and cream over them and add a ladle of the stock in which the lungs were cooked. Stir the bread into the lungs mixture. If it is too thick, add some milk or stock. Bake the *mežerli* in a large pan, baking tray or shallow, round clay bowl (in Slovenia known as a "*štecl*"). Grease the bowl, put the mixture into it and bake in a medium hot over for 45 minutes. When it is done, the *mežerli* develops a savoury yellowish crust. Serve with a salad.

Wine: dry or medium dry white wines from Štajerska, such as Mariborčan or Ljutomerčan, or single variety wines such as Šipon, Laški Rizling or Chardonnay

Kulinji

I N G R E D I E N T S:

500 g flour

3-4 eggs

100 g fat

200 ml cream

a handful of poppy seeds

Make the dough as for *rezanci* (the recipe is on page 76). Roll out the dough and cut it into 4 x 4 cm squares. Boil some water in a pot, add salt, then cook the dough squares. Strain off the *kulinji* and fry them in the fat.

Serve with cream and sprinkled with poppy seeds.

92

Tunjka Pork and Sausages

(see picture)

The traditional Slovenian *tunjka* is a small wooden barrel with a lid in which pork is preserved in lard. Any meat that is intended to be preserved in this way must be fresh, cold, firm and of the highest quality.

Remove the bone and cut the meat into pieces of whatever size you desire. Large pieces are unsuitable because once the meat is removed from the preserve it has to be used at once. Spice and dress the meat as for ordinary roast pork: salt each piece and rub in garlic, caraway seeds, lemon juice, etc. Roast the meat slowly and thoroughly in the oven. Baste while roasting to prevent burning. When the meat is done, allow to cool.

An earthen or stone vessel can be used instead of the wooden *tunjka*. Pour some molten fat into the *tunjka* a few fingers deep, then allow to cool and harden. Place the cold pieces of meat next to each other on the fat, but make sure that they are not packed too tightly. Pour more molten lard over the meat and make sure that it fills all the empty spaces between the pieces. The layer of fat covering the meat should be a few fingers thick. Make several such alternate layers of meat and fat until all the meat is used. Seal with a top layer of pure lard. Allow to cool completely then cover the fat with cellophane, cling-film or greaseproof paper. Finally, tightly close the cask with the lid and store in a dark, cool larder.

Meat preserved in this way keeps for several months. Each time some meat is removed from the tunjka, the cask must be carefully resealed. Dried or fresh meat as well as sausages, including blood sausages, can be preserved in a similar way; liver sausage, however, should be sealed immediately after boiling and cooling, and fried prior to use.

Wine: mature dry white Štajerska wines, e.g. Šipon, Laški Rizling, Beli Pinot or Chardonnay

Frogs' Legs Prekmurje Style

(see picture)

INGREDIENTS:

60 frogs' legs
150 g fat
250 g onions
300 ml sour cream
1 tsp of sweet paprika
a sprig of parsley
salt

Clean and thoroughly rinse the frogs' legs; chop the onions and parsley. Fry the legs in the fat, add fried onions and sprinkle with chopped parsley and paprika, then add the sour cream and salt. Cover the pot and braise until the frogs' legs soften. Remove them from the pot, arrange in a bowl and add the sauce. If the sauce is too thin, allow to thicken on the stove.

Serve with buckwheat porridge (p. 100), *kulinji* (without the poppy seeds, page 92) or potato and spinach dumplings (page 139).

Wine: dry or medium dry white wines from the Drava Valley region

Partridge Prekmurje Style

INGREDIENTS:

1 partridge
50 g smoked bacon
50 g onions
2 cloves garlic
50 ml sour cream
10 g flour
120 g *mlinci* (see page 88)
30 g pork crackling
a few sprigs of parsley
sweet paprika (to taste)
a pinch of caraway seeds
a bay leaf

Marinate the partridge for 4-5 days; clean it, then wrap and tie in a large long slice of smoked bacon. Chop the remaining bacon and the onions; fry this together with the onion in a pan, then place the partridge on top. Cover the pan and braise until the partridge softens. When it is done, put the bird into a fresh pot. Add some flour, crushed or chopped garlic, caraway seeds and the bay leaf to the pan with the onion. When it releases its aroma, sprinkle with paprika, add the sour cream and allow to boil. Finally blend the sauce and, depending on taste, dilute with marinade or stock. Halve the partridge, and return it to the sauce.

In the meantime, heat a pot containing a litre of water, add salt and bring to the boil. Pour the boiling water over the *mlinci* (see page 88), then garnish them with pork crackling. Serve the partridge and sauce on a plate together with the mlinci.

Wine: dry or medium dry white wine, e.g. Sivi Pinot or Rulandec

Štajerska Bean Goulash

I N G R E D I E N T S :

1.5 kg dried beans (seeds)	
300 g smoked pork	
200 g fresh pork	
100 g fat	
4 onions	
2 cloves garlic	
1 tsp of sweet paprika	
2 bay leaves	
1 carrot	
50 g tomato purée	
salt	

Soak the dried bean seeds overnight; boil in slightly salted water. While the beans are cooking, finely chop the onions and garlic, cut the meat and grate the carrot. Fry the onion and garlic in the fat; when they release an aroma, add the meat, paprika, bay leaves and grated carrot. Braise until the meat softens. Then add it to the beans, salt, and allow to boil. Finally, add the tomato purée and cook a little more.

Wine: a rosé or young red wine, e.g. Modra Frankinja, Modra Portugalka, or. Žametna Črnina from the indigenous Žametovka grape

Bujta Repa

(Pork with Pickled Grated Turnips)

(see picture, below)

I N G R E D I E N T S :

1 kg *kisla repa* (pickled grated turnip)	
1.5 kg loin or pork	
250 millet groats	
100 g fat	
50 g flour	
5 cloves garlic	
1 onion	
salt	
100 ml sour cream	

Boil the pork with the *kisla repa* in barely enough water to cover both. When the *kisla repa* is almost done, add the washed and sorted millet groats and boil.

Make a roux from the fat and flour, then stir in the chopped onions and garlic. Dilute with some cold water, add it to the *kisla repa* and groats, then let it come to the boil; this both thickens the dish and improves the flavour. Add sour cream and salt to taste. A mixture of sour cream and flour can be used instead of the roux. When the *kisla repa* and pork soften, remove the pork and cut it into slices. If the pork is from a young animal, it will be ready before the *kisla repa*, so remove it from the pot and continue cooking the *kisla repa* by itself. Put the cooked turnip into a bowl and place the slices of pork on top.

Serve as an individual dish.

Smoked pork can also be used instead of fresh pork.

Wine: dry white Prekmurje wine, Šipon, Zeleni Silvanec

Roast Lamb with Baked Turnips

INGREDIENTS:

1.5 kg lamb with bones
400 g turnips
400 g potatoes
100 g fat
a ladle of stock
2 cloves garlic
a pinch of thyme
pepper
a pinch of caraway seeds
salt

Wash the lamb thoroughly, wipe and rub in the salt and herbs. Place onto a baking tray and pour molten fat over it. Add a ladle of stock and roast in a preheated oven. Baste the meat with its own juices several times during roasting. The meat should be ready in approximately one hour.

Clean and peel the turnips and potatoes and slice. Put into a pot and add enough water to barely cover the vegetables. Add the caraway seeds and salt, then cook until almost done. Strain, add to the meat in the baking tray and roast until done.

Wine: rosé or dry red wines, e.g. Modra Frankinja or Modri Pinot

Horseradish Jelly

INGREDIENTS:

1 cup of milk
2 tbsp butter
2 tbsp flour
salt
100 g grated horseradish
2 sour apples
2 tbsp breadcrumbs
salt
1/2 lemon
a small bunch of chives
1 red pepper
3 leaves gelatine

Make a béchamel sauce from the butter, flour and milk. Salt, then add the grated horseradish, grated apples, breadcrumbs and lemon juice to the hot sauce. Stir until smooth. Finally, add the chopped chives, diced red pepper and the gelatine dissolved in a little water. Stir to distribute the gelatine evenly into the sauce. Pour the mix into a shallow mould rinsed with cold water, then place it into a refrigerator to harden.

Baked Smoked Ham in Pastry

(see picture)

INGREDIENTS:

1 smoked ham	
flour	
water	
yeast	
a pinch of caraway seeds	
a bay leaf	

Prepare a nice smoked ham. Ready the yeast and mix it with the flour and water to form a pastry dough. Knead the crushed caraway seeds and bay leaf into the dough. Cover with a cloth and allow to rise. Roll out the pastry, put the ham onto it and then wrap the pastry around the ham. Put into a greased baking tin and bake at moderate temperature — roughly 1 hour of baking per 1 kg of ham, depending on how strongly the ham has been smoked. Cut slices from the hot or cold ham, depending on taste.
Serve with horseradish jelly.

Wine: rosé or dry red wines, e.g. Modri Pinot or Modra Frankinja

99

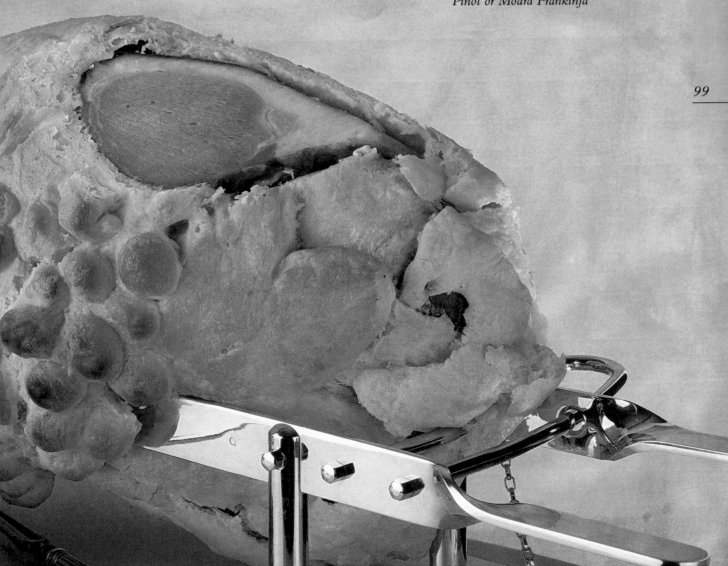

Štajerska Baked Štruklji

(see picture)

INGREDIENTS:

Pastry

500 g flour

1 egg

salt

1 tbsp oil

a little lukewarm water

Filling

150 ml cream

250 g cottage cheese

1 egg

1 kg peeled and grated apples

100 g sugar

50 g raisins

1 tsp cinnamon

breadcrumbs (to thicken the filling)

Make a filo pastry dough from the flour, egg, oil, salt and water and allow to rest for 30 minutes.

Prepare the filling: mash the cottage cheese and add the cream, egg yolk and cinnamon. Whisk the egg white and fold it carefully into the filling.

Roll out and stretch the dough across a broad flour-covered cloth, spread the filling over it and sprinkle with grated apples, sugar, raisins and breadcrumbs. It the filling is too thin, add more breadcrumbs. By lifting the cloth, roll up the pastry and filling into a roulade. Place the *štruklji* onto a greased baking tray and bake for about 40 minutes in a moderate oven.

Wine: Chardonnay, Renski Rizling, Sauvignon

Vrtanek Bread

INGREDIENTS:

1 kg flour

0.5 l sour milk

50 g yeast

ground pepper

40 g butter (for greasing tray)

Vrtanek is a specially prepared large loaf of bread made from quality flour. Traditionally it is an integral part of all banquets, weddings and important festivities in this part of Slovenia.

Break up the yeast, mix with a teaspoon of sugar, two tablespoons of flour and warm water, and allow to rise in a warm place. Sift the flour into a bowl, add the sour milk, yeast solution and some pepper, then knead thoroughly. Cover with a cloth and allow to rise slowly in a warm place. Knead the dough again and divide it into three equal loaves. Shape them into strands and plait them into a braid; then form the braid into a dough garland. Place the garland onto a round greased baking tray and decorate with pieces of dough. Cover with a cloth and allow to rise again in a warm place. Brush with whisked egg and bake in a preheated oven.

Buckwheat Porridge

INGREDIENTS:

400 ml buckwheat groats

1.5 l milk

salt

cream

Salt the milk and boil. Wash the groats then add them to the boiling milk and cook until tender. Add salt and cream, to taste.

Serve with milk.

Prekmurje Gibanica Pie

INGREDIENTS:

Flan Pastry for base

250 g flour

80 g butter

1 egg

2-3 tbsp cream

a pinch of salt

1 tsp sugar

Filo Pastry for layers

400 g flour

1 egg

2 tbsp oil

a dash of vinegar or lemon juice

a little lukewarm water

a pinch of salt

Poppy Seed Filling

200 g ground poppy seeds

50 g sugar

1 sachet vanilla sugar

approx. 100 ml milk or cream

1 egg

Cottage Cheese Filling

400 g cottage cheese

1 egg

100 ml thick sour cream

50 g raisins

50 g sugar

Walnut Filling

200 g ground walnuts

50 g sugar

1 sachet vanilla sugar

cinnamon (to taste)

100-200 ml milk

Apple Filling

500 g apples

30 g sugar

grated peel of 1 lemon

cinnamon (to taste)

fat for greasing the baking tin

a little butter

cream for topping (to taste)

Prekmurje Gibanica is made from two types of pastry: flan and filo. The flan pastry is used to cover the bottom of the deep baking dish or tin — the dough at the base must be harder because the *gibanica* is heavy.

Mix all the ingredients for the flan pastry in a bowl. Knead thoroughly until the dough is smooth; allow to rest for 30 minutes.

Prepare the filo pastry: mix all the ingredients into a dough, make several smaller loaves and allow them to rest for 30 minutes.

While the doughs are resting, prepare the fillings:

Poppy Seed Filling: grind the seeds, scald with boiling milk; add sugar, spices and vanilla sugar, then mix.

Cottage Cheese Filling: break up the cottage cheese with a fork; add the egg, cream, washed raisins and sugar. Mix thoroughly.

Walnut Filling: grind the walnuts and scald with milk; add sugar, vanilla sugar and cinnamon then mix. This filling must be a smooth paste.

Apple Filling: peel the apples, cut into thin slices, then stew with sugar. Add the cinnamon and grated lemon peel.

Roll out the more brittle flan pastry dough to half a centimetre thickness, and use it to line a greased baking dish, preferably an earthen one. The dough must stretch over the edge of the dish.

Sprinkle some flour over a cloth and stretch the filo pastry dough very thinly over it and allow to dry a little.

Now one can start composing the *gibanica*. Spread a one centimetre-thick layer of poppy seed filling on the flan pastry, cover with a sheet of filo pastry, then sprinkle with some melted butter. Spread the cottage cheese filling over the filo pastry and cover with another piece of filo pastry; and again sprinkle with melted butter. Spread the walnut filling over this leaf, cover with another leaf of filo pastry and sprinkle with butter. Make a layer of apple filling, cover it with another piece of filo pastry and sprinkle with more butter. Repeat the whole process again. Cover the final layer of filling with one or two leaves of filo pastry and sprinkle with butter. Finally, spread some cream over the *gibanica* and bake in a moderate preheated oven for approximately one hour.

Wine: Traminec, Rulandec or Rumeni Muškat

Prleška Gibanica

(Savoury Gibanica from Prlekija)

(see picture)

INGREDIENTS:

Pastry

400 g flour

a little lukewarm water

salt

1-2 eggs (optional)

Filling

1.25 kg cottage cheese

3 eggs yolks

0.5 l sour cream

200 g butter or margarine

salt

Make a filo pastry from the flour, water and salt, knead thoroughly and allow to rest. While the dough is resting, prepare the filling: mash the cottage cheese with a fork, add the egg yolks and salt. Sprinkle some flour over a cloth and stretch the filo pastry over it very thinly, then allow it to dry a little. Take a round baking tin and cut nine round discs in the dough. Line the bottom of the greased baking tin with the first dough disc. The pastry must stretch over the edge of the tin. Spread molten butter and cream over it, then cover with another disc of filo pastry and spread the cottage cheese filling over it.

Cover with a new layer, sprinkle with molten butter and spread another layer of cottage cheese. Repeat until all the pieces of filo pastry have been used. Fold the edge of the bottom-most disc over the final layer of filling and cover with the last layer of pastry.

Mix some cream and egg yolk and pour over the *gibanica*. Bake in a preheated oven at a moderate temperature until light brown.

Wine: Laški Rizling, Zeleni Silvanec, Sauvignon, Chardonnay, Beli Pinot

Buckwheat Gibanica

INGREDIENTS:

Pastry

1 kg buckwheat flour

0.5 l water

3 tbsp butter

Filling

150 g butter

4 eggs

500 g cottage cheese

2 tbsp cream

2 ladles milk or cream

salt

Boil the water, add salt and fat. Put the flour into a bowl and pour the water into it. Knead the mixture into a dough and roll out very thinly. Mix the butter and eggs, add the mashed cottage cheese and cream. Sugar can also be added if a sweet *gibanica* is preferred.

Spread the filling over the rolled pastry, roll into a roulade and place in a well greased baking tin. Bake in a preheated oven. Pour the cream and milk over the *gibanica* while it is baking.

Wine: as for the previous gibanica

105

Prekmurje Krapci

I N G R E D I E N T S:

Dough

600 g flour

40 g yeast (and a little sugar)

100–150 g fat

5–6 tbsp milk

a pinch of salt

Filling

1 kg cottage cheese

500 g millet meal

1–1.5 l milk

2 eggs

sugar (to taste)

cinnamon (to taste)

cream (optional)

salt

Mix the broken yeast, a teaspoon of sugar, two teaspoons of flour and 100 ml lukewarm water, then stir before allowing to rise. Put the flour into a bowl, add fat, salt, the yeast and lukewarm milk, and knead into a dough. Allow the dough to rise in a warm place. Prepare the filling: clean the millet thoroughly and cook in slightly salted milk. When the millet is done, remove from the heat and allow to cool. Add the cottage cheese, eggs, cream and spices. Do not add sugar: the sugar should be sprinkled over the *krapci* when they are done. If preferred, the yolks can be mixed into the filling, and the beaten egg whites folded in later.

Roll the dough out to the thickness of one finger, sprinkle with flour and put into a greased baking tin. The edge rim of the dough should be thicker than the rest so that the filling does not spill over the side. Spread the filling over the dough. Let the cake rise for 15–20 minutes (it must be at least 6 cm high) then put into a preheated oven. Pour cream over the filling several times during baking. When the *krapci* is done, pour some more cream over the filling and leave in the oven for a few minutes to soak. Cut into 8 by 10 cm or 6 by 10 cm slices.

Wine: dry or medium dry white wines from the Drava Valley region

Walnut Potica

(see picture)

INGREDIENTS:

Dough

600 g flour

40 g yeast

2 tbsp lukewarm milk

2 tbsp flour

1 tsp sugar

2 egg yolks

50 g butter

50 g sugar

200–300 ml milk

peel of 1 lemon

salt

Filling

300–400 g walnuts

200 ml milk

lemon peel

1 tsp cinnamon

2 tbsp rum

100 g sugar

100 g honey

2 egg whites

40 g butter

Sift the flour into a bowl, cover, and put in a warm place. Prepare the yeast: mix fresh yeast with two tablespoons of lukewarm milk, add two tablespoons of flour and a teaspoon of sugar then stir and allow to rise in a warm place. In the meantime, whisk the fat, egg yolks or whole eggs and sugar. Warm the milk gently, add salt, grated lemon peel and the prepared mixture of fat, eggs and sugar; allow to cool. Make a dough from the warmed flour, milk and yeast mixture (do not use all the milk at once, add it gradually and only if and when nec-essary). Knead and beat the dough until it no longer sticks to the bowl, then cover it with a cloth and put it in a warm place to rise.

In the meantime, prepare the filling. Pour the milk into the pan, add the butter and half the sugar and bring to the boil; use the hot mixture to scald the walnuts. Warm the honey separately and add it to the walnuts, together with the grated lemon peel, cinnamon and rum. Let the mixture cool. Beat the egg whites and the remaining sugar until hard and fold carefully into the filling.

When the dough has doubled in size, roll it out to the thickness of one finger. Spread the filling over it and roll into a tight roulade, then place the *potica* in a greased baking tin. Allow to rise again in a warm place.

Whisk an egg, spread it over the cake and bake for approximately one hour in a preheated oven. When it is done, remove the *potica* from the baking tin immediately to prevent the crust from becoming moist and breaking away from the rest of the cake.

Bizeljsko Buckwheat Potica

INGREDIENTS:

Dough

300 g buckwheat flour	
300 g wheat flour	
0.5 l water	
salt	
50 g sugar	
50 g butter	
20 g yeast	
5 tbsp milk	
2 tbsp wheat flour	
2 tbsp sugar	

Filling

500 g cottage cheese	
100 ml thick cream	
100 g sugar	
2 whipped egg whites	
2 egg yolks	
50–100 g raisins	
100 g walnuts	
a pinch of cinnamon	

First activate the yeast and put into a warm place to rise.

Sift the buckwheat flour into a bowl. Boil the water, add salt, butter and sugar, then pour this mixture into the buckwheat flour. Stir thoroughly and allow to cool, then add the yeast and wheat flour. Knead thoroughly until the dough no longer sticks to the bowl or fingers. Cover the dough with a cloth and put in a warm place to rise.

Prepare the filling: mash the cottage cheese, add the cream, egg yolks, sugar and cinnamon. Beat the egg whites until hard and fold lightly into the filling. Sprinkle some flour onto a broad cloth and roll the dough out thinly. Spread the filling over the dough and sprinkle with raisins and/or walnuts. Use the cloth to help roll the dough into a roll cake, then place it into a greased baking tin. Allow the *potica* to rise, but not too much; put it into a preheated oven and bake.

In the autumn, fresh grapes can be used instead of raisins.

Farmer's Bread Potica

INGREDIENTS:

Dough

100-150 g soft white flour

lukewarm water

4 tbsp oil

salt

Filling

10 eggs

1 l thick cream

1.5 kg good cottage cheese

750 g white bread

0.5 l milk

a pinch of cinnamon

2 tbsp sugar

Put the flour into a bowl, add lukewarm water, oil and salt, then knead thoroughly for 15 minutes. Form into a loaf and cover with a cloth, then allow to rest for 30 minutes. Cut the bread into thin slices and soak in the milk. Whisk the eggs and stir the cottage cheese to give it a homogeneous texture. Roll the dough out thinly and line a greased baking tin with it, allowing the mass to extend over the edge of the tin. Brush some whisked egg over the dough, cover with a layer of soaked bread, then pour some egg over it. Continue with a layer of warmed cottage cheese, pour some warmed cream over it, and sprinkle with sugar and cinnamon. Repeat the procedure again and complete the *potica* with a layer of bread. Pull the dough extending over the edge of the tin over the top, and pinch off the thick edges to close. Brush some whisked egg over the *potica* and bake in a hot preheated oven for approximately 45 minutes.

Poppy Seed Povitica

(see picture)

INGREDIENTS:

Dough

1 kg flour

30 g yeast

3 eggs

2 tbsp sugar

8-10 tbsp cream

300 ml milk

salt

1 egg

Filling

400 g ground poppy seeds

100-200 ml milk

200 g sugar

100 g butter or fat

100 ml cream

2 eggs

Sift the flour into a bowl and add salt. Mix the yeast with a teaspoon of sugar, two tablespoons of flour and 50 ml lukewarm water or milk and allow to rise in a warm place.

Make a depression in the middle of the flour and pour in the whisked eggs, yeast, cream and sugar. Add lukewarm milk while stirring the mixture. Continue beating the dough until bubbles start forming, and it no longer sticks to the bowl or ladle. Sprinkle with flour, cover with a cloth and allow to rise in a warm place.

Prepare the filling: cook the poppy seeds for approximately 25 minutes in the milk and cream and stir continuously. Mix and stir the butter, sugar and eggs in another dish. Add the cooled poppy seeds to this mixture. Cinnamon and vanilla sugar can also be added, depending on taste. Stir the mixture.

Roll the dough out — about half a centimetre thick — sprinkle with flour and spread the filling over it evenly. Roll into a tight roulade and put into a greased baking tin. Cover with a cloth and put in a warm place to rise again. Brush with a whisked egg and bake in a preheated oven.

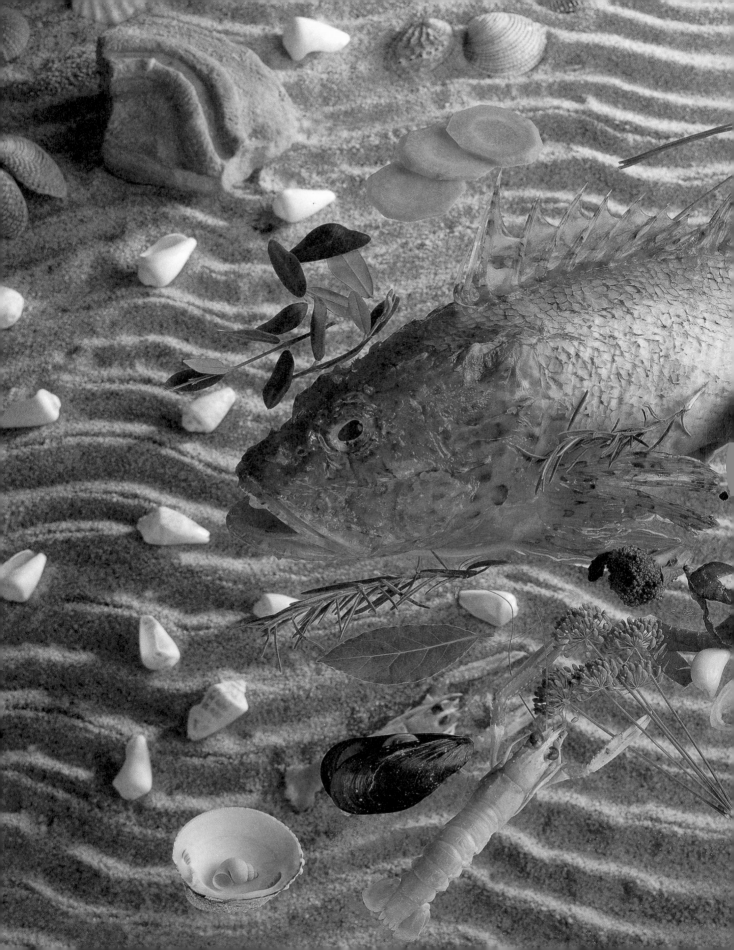

Primorska
and
Notranjska
Dishes

Primorska and Notranjska

The name *Primorska* (the coastal region) has come to signify the entire western part of Slovenia, although it includes only about 40 km of coastline. Another 40 km could be added to this if one takes into account the coast north of the Trieste pocket, where the present-day international border runs so very close to the coast, and where Slovenian people have lived (as the names of the villages bear witness) since time immemorial. As one might expect, seafood becomes less frequent as one leaves the coast and heads further into the interior of Primorska. At the same time the "gentle breeze" that blows inland from the Mediterranean grows gradually weaker, finally dying away completely in the Alpine valleys to the northwest.

Primorska can thus be subdivided into the Adriatic coastal strip and the interior, which comprises numerous highland plateaus, the perforated Karst and the abounding Vipava Valley. This is a bright, blossoming land, the cultural peculiarities of which have been influenced by the Mediterranean Roman world to the west.

Along the coast, however, the situation was quite different. The town nuclei of Piran, Koper, Izola and, of course, Trieste and Muggia, retained their ancient Latin character; nevertheless, the entire rural hinterland, up to the gates of the towns themselves, has been Slovenian for a millennium. The symbiotic rela-

tionship between the rural and urban elements of the coastal population gave rise to an animated mercantile and cultural exchange and, because gastronomy is a primeval constituent of any culture, there was centuries-long culinary intercourse between them. In the Istrian hinterland, where Slovenian, Croatian, Italian and other influences meet, administrative and parish boundaries were constantly changing, making the interaction and the exchange of culinary habits even more direct. The prevailing characteristics of this relatively diverse gastronomy are, therefore, Mediterranean boldness and wit in seasoning with herbs, especially exotic ones such as cinnamon and, whenever possible, cloves. The copious use of gar-

lic, which is not only salubrious, but also imparts a very good flavour to the food, the application of olive oil as a dressing, especially with fish, as well as some rather daring combinations of flavours are all also fairly typical. Illustrative of this are the sweet blood sausages (black puddings) from the Vipava Valley known as *mulce*, the filling of which not only includes the classic ingredients such as meat, entrails, blood, pepper, marjoram and parsley, but also raisins, cinnamon, apples, oranges and even pine kernels and sugar. The logic behind creating such an unusual dish was probably quite simple: oranges, pine kernels and raisins were foods usually reserved for the gentry, and adding these to blood sausages — a simple traditional dish — would

make the latter more festive, especially since such a combination was perfectly acceptable to Mediterranean culinary principles.

At the other extreme, poverty, as elsewhere in Slovenia, inspired the imagination and led to the creation of some interesting savoury dishes made from the simplest of ingredients. Who could have imagined that good "spinach", which the locals refer to as *"višče"* (foliage) could have been made from turnip shoots? And what of *zelševka* — a variation of the ubiquitous *potica* cake from the town of Idrija — made from chives, onion shoots, young yarrow, mint and tarragon. A similar dish, but even more diverse in its ingredients, is prepared in the Brda district for

Easter — all sorts of "weeds" are collected to prepare this herbal pie. And, finally, in this bracket one should also include the renowned *jota*, which is a thick soup containing pickled turnips, kidney beans, potatoes, sour cream and sometimes bacon or other cured meat, garlic and tomatoes as well as a medley of spices. In Primorska a good cook is distinguished from a bad one by the quality of her *jota*. Primorska *mineštra* (minestrone) can be just as varied — from a *ričet* (barley porridge boiled with beans and containing sauerkraut and pork) to a vegetable hot-pot; maize (corn) *ričet* — a dish that resembles the Serbian *pasulj,* but containing beans, kohlrabi and potatoes — is known as *Primorska trojka. Pašta*, on the other

hand, was borrowed from Italy, as the name quite clearly indicates.

Festive occasions in Primorska are customarily marked by the serving of *pinca*, a sweet bread with a high butter content. *Pinca* is the standard Easter cake in Primorska; in the Postojna area it is known as *"župnik"* (the parish priest). One of the parade horses of the cuisine of Primorska is certainly *gubanica*, a cake made from chocolate, almonds, walnuts, pine kernels, candied orange peel, lemons, raisins, rum, maraschino liqueur, vanilla, wine, butter and two types of dough.

The cuisine of Primorska is definitely one of the pearls of Slovenian cooking.

The Vineyards and Wines of the Primorska Region

This region extends from the western part of the country, adjacent to the Italian border, to the far southwest of Slovenia, and the Adriatic coast around the port of Koper. The Mediterranean climate provides the wines with an abundance of sun and warmth. Diversity is also a characteristic of this region; its four districts contain one-third of all Slovenia's vineyards, which yield some two-fifths of all the nation's wine. In the *Brda district* white varieties prevail, with the *Vipava district* boasting a few less, the *Koper district* only a handful and the *Karst district* even fewer. Primorska is renowned for its excellent red and rosé wines, but it also produces very rich and full white wines, which are almost exclusively all dry. *Rebula* and *Malvazija* (Malvasier) are the traditional Primorska white varieties, although *Chardonnay, Beli Pinot* (Pinot Blanc), *Sivi Pinot* (Pinot Gris), *Sauvignon* and *Laški Rizling* (Italian Riesling) vines are also grown. The Vipava district also produces wines from the traditional and indigenous *Zelen* and *Pinela* vines, whilst *"Tokaj"*, made from a vine related to Mus-

cat, as well as wines from the *Pikolit* grape are made in the Brda district. Of the red varieties, the most common are *Merlot, Refošk* (Refosco) and *Cabernet Sauvignon*. Some *Cabernet Franc* and *Barbera* is also produced.

Kraški Teran (made from the Refosco grape grown on the iron-rich *terra rossa* soil of the Karst region) and *Koprski Refošk* (made from the Refosco grape in the Koper winery) are almost obligatory when cured meats dried in the cool dry winds of the high Karst are served. Game, on the other hand, is accompanied by mature red wines like *Teranton* (a fully matured barrique Teran) and *Merlot Barrique* (a wine also aged in oak casks).

Jota

(see picture)

INGREDIENTS:

500 g dried kidney beans (seeds)
500 g potatoes
500 g sauerkraut
150 g cured bacon
1 onion
50 g flour
garlic
a bay leaf
1 tomato
salt
(a little cured neck of pork — optional)

Clean and wash the beans and allow them to soak overnight. Cook the beans, potatoes and sauerkraut separately. Chop the bacon and onions. Fry the bacon on a high heat and fry the onions with it until they turn yellow. Stir in the flour and continue frying, then add water and cook until smooth. Add the beans, potatoes and sauerkraut together with the water in which they were cooked. Spice with the bay leaf and crushed garlic, then add the tomato and, finally, salt. Cook until the soup boils strongly and serve. If some neck of pork is added, it should be cooked with the sauerkraut. When it is done, cut into pieces and put it into the *jota* to boil a little more. *Jota* can also be prepared with *kisla repa* (pickled grated turnips). In this case, mash the potatoes and add chopped garlic. Finally, add the sour cream before serving.

Jota is good even when reheated.

Wine: rosé

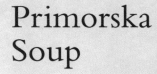

Primorska Soup

INGREDIENTS:

100 g olive oil
1 onion
3 tbsp flour
5 tbsp tomato purée
200 g pasta
200 g grated cheese
a sprig of parsley
a bay leaf
water
salt

Finely chop the onion and fry in some oil until yellow. Add the flour and make a light roux; then add water to make it a soupy consistency. Season with salt, stir in the tomato purée, the bay leaf and pasta and cook. Boil the pasta in the soup, but ensure that it does not overcook. Garnish with grated cheese and chopped parsley before serving.

Čompe

(Potatoes with Cottage Cheese)

INGREDIENTS:

1 kg potatoes

500 g cottage cheese

Wash the potatoes thoroughly, halve and cook them (unpeeled) in salted water.
Strain and serve with fresh, home-made cottage cheese.

Wine: rosé

Pašta Fižol

(Pasta with Beans)

INGREDIENTS:

1 kg dried kidney beans (seeds)

750 g pasta

150 g dry cured pork

50 g flour

1 small onion

a clove of garlic

a few tbsp of tomato purée

marjoram (to taste)

a bay leaf

salt

pepper

sweet paprika (to taste)

a dash of vinegar

Clean and wash the beans thoroughly, soak them overnight, then boil them until tender. Cook the pasta separately (do not overdo), strain and rinse in cold water. Chop the pork and fry in oil. Add the chopped onion and continue frying until yellow, then add the flour, crushed garlic and tomato purée. Stir in enough water to make a smooth sauce. Pour the sauce onto the unstrained beans, then add the pasta. Season with salt, paprika, pepper, the bay leaf and marjoram. Allow to boil for some time, then add vinegar. The consistency of this dish must be fairly thick.

Pasta with beans can be improved considerably if meat stock is used or if a piece of dried meat is cooked with the beans.

Wine: dry white or rosé wines

Primorska Trojka

INGREDIENTS:

500 g potatoes

500 g yellow kohlrabi

500 g dried kidney beans (seeds)

750 dried pork

100–150 g pork crackling

salt

a dash of vinegar

Clean and wash the beans, then soak in water overnight to rehydrate. Cook the dried pork with the beans in the water they were soaked in. When the beans are half cooked, add sliced of diced kohlrabi and, after a while, the diced potatoes. Remove the meat from the pot when it softens. Add salt to the dish if necessary and mash. Dress with the pork crackling. Depending on taste, vinegar may be added just prior to removing the dish from the heat.

Cut the meat into pieces and mix it into the dish, or serve separately. The *trojka* can be dressed and thickened with a roux made from fat and flour. Chopped onions, parsley and crushed garlic can also be added to this roux.

Wine: light red Primorska wines or young red wines

Primorska Minestrone

(see picture)

INGREDIENTS:

2 l water

1 kg assorted vegetables: cauliflower, celery, carrots, leek, cabbage, yellow kohlrabi, etc.

50 g cured bacon

2 tbsp oil

1 onion

4 tbsp rice

2 tbsp tomato purée or 5 fresh tomatoes

2 tbsp grated Parmesan cheese

Clean and wash the vegetables, then dice finely. Cut the bacon into small pieces and finely chop the onion. Heat some oil in a saucepan, fry the bacon and add the onion. Cook until it turns yellow, add the vegetables followed by the peeled and chopped tomatoes; stir fry for 10 minutes then add water and allow to simmer. When the vegetables are almost done, mix in the rice, tomato purée (optional) and salt. Garnish with the grated Parmesan before serving.

Wine: dry white Primorska wines, Rebula

Friko

(see picture, below)

INGREDIENTS:

400 g potatoes
600 g cheese
500 g fat bacon or lard
4 eggs
salt

Wash and peel the potatoes. Cut into thin slices, add salt and fry in hot fat or chopped fatty bacon. Whisk the eggs, add diced cheese and stir into the potatoes. When the eggs harden on one side, turn the *friko* over and fry the other side. Larger quantities can be baked in the oven or fried in several goes. Serve with *polenta*, bread or salad.

Wine: Barbera or Teran wine

Primorska Višče

(see picture, top right)

INGREDIENTS:

a bunch of young turnip leaves
80 g butter
3-4 cloves garlic
1 tbsp parsley
3 tbsp meat stock
salt

Select nice young turnip leaves, wash thoroughly and remove the stalks. Simmer them in a little water in a saucepan. When they are half cooked, chop them. Stir-fry the crushed garlic and parsley in butter, add the chopped turnip leaves, stock and salt and allow to boil. Serve as a side dish.

Idrija Žlikrofi

(see picture at top of page 125)

INGREDIENTS:

Dough

500 g flour
3 egg yolks and 100 ml milk; or
3 eggs and a little less than 100 ml milk;
50 g oil or fat for dressing
50 g breadcrumbs (optional)

Filling

3 cooked potatoes
50 g lard or minced bacon fat
3 egg whites or 3 whole eggs
breadcrumbs
cinnamon
parsley
marjoram
pepper

Make a dough from the flour, egg yolks or whole eggs and milk; the dough should be softer than that used for *rezanci*. Knead into a loaf, cover and allow to rest for 30 minutes. To make the filling, cook the potatoes, strain, peel and mash whilst still hot. Add some fat or minced lard, egg whites or whole eggs, breadcrumbs, pepper, cinnamon, chopped parsley and marjoram. Mix all the ingredients into a smooth mixture.

Hashed meat can also be added to the filling, in which case fewer potatoes should be used. Roll out the rested dough thinly. Place spoonfuls of filling evenly on the dough and cut around them. Brush some egg white on the edges of the dough surrounding the filling. Bring together the dough from opposite sides and, using the eggs as an adhesive, pinch them together above the filling to make a pocket. Taking care not to damage the dough, make a small depression in the dough above the filling; in this way the *žlikrofi* obtain their characteristic hat-like appearance. Cook the *žlikrofi* in salted boiling water. If salt was added to the filling, the water should not be too salty. Bring to the boil and cook gently for 10–15 minutes. Strain carefully, put into a bowl and dress with hot fat.

Žlikrofi are best served with *bakalca* (see page 125) or other meats with gravy. They can also be served as an individual dish with a salad, in which case they should be garnished with breadcrumbs fried in oil.

Wine: Rebula or fresh dry white wines, e.g. Chardonnay

123

Žvarcet

INGREDIENTS:

INGREDIENTS:

1.5 kg veal

100 g butter

50 g breadcrumbs

water or beef stock

marjoram

lemon peel

nutmeg

a little grated Parmesan cheese

salt

Cut the meat into pieces and braise in its own juices in a pan. When the juice evaporates, fry the bread-crumbs in butter in a frying pan and add them to the meat. Pour in enough water to cover the meat, then season with salt, marjoram, lemon peel and nutmeg. Cook gently on a low heat for 30 minutes. Sprinkle some grated Parmesan cheese over the dish and serve. Serve with *polenta*, *žganci*, pasta or rice.

Wine: Beli Pinot, Chardonnay

124

Bakalca

(see picture, bottom)

INGREDIENTS:

1.5 kg mutton
50 g butter
3 onions
4 carrots
a clove of garlic
a bay leaf
a sprig of thyme
a few peppercorns
a few cloves
vinegar or white wine (optional)
2 tbsp flour
salt

Cut the meat into pieces. Clean the carrots and cut them into discs. Cut the onions and garlic into thin slices. Fry the onions, garlic and carrots in fat, then add meat and stir-fry. Add enough water to cover the meat, the bay leaf, thyme, pepper, cloves, salt and some vinegar or wine. Let the dish simmer until the meat softens. Sprinkle with a little flour and cook some more; then add a little more vinegar or wine (to taste), and bring to a boil.

Serve the *bakalca* with Idrija *žlikrofi* (see page 123).

Wine: the same wine as was used to make the dish is appropriate; e.g. white wine from the Primorska region

Pršut

(Primorska Prosciutto)

(see picture)

Prepare a mixture of crushed garlic, salt, pepper, bay leaves and rosemary. Rub this mixture very thoroughly into the ham (upper leg) joint of a one-year-old pig. Place the ham in a dish and leave to stand for three to four days, depending on the size of the joint. Do not add any water. Put the leg between two boards and place a heavy weight on the upper one to squeeze the fluid out.

Once again, heavily sprinkle the ham with pepper and other spices. Using a finger, separate the bone from the meat and fill in the space along the femur with salt, crushed garlic and pepper. Rub crushed garlic around the bone itself. Hang the joint up to cure in dry air; best of all for this purpose is the dry cold bora wind of Slovenia's Karst region. Cure the meat for 10–11 months. Serve with olives and white bread.

Wine: Teran

Kraške Mulce

(Karst Style Blood Sausages)

I N G R E D I E N T S:

2 kg fatty meat
1 whole pig lung
pig's intestines
500 g white bread
3-4 apples
1.5 l blood
250 g raisins
100 g pine kernels
500 g sugar
salt
pepper
marjoram (to taste)

Cook the meat and lungs separately, mince into small pieces then make a hash. Cut the bread into small cubes, soak in the meat stock, strain and add to the meat. Cook the apples, strain, then mash together with the meat. Thoroughly stir in the fresh blood (collected during slaughter and stirred). Also stir the raisins, pine kernels, sugar, salt, pepper and marjoram into the mixture, which should then be stuffed into cleaned and washed intestines to form sausages. Carefully boil the sausages for 15 minutes; remove from the heat and place first in cold water, then on a board to cool.

Fry the sausages in some fat prior to serving.

The *mulce* will be softer if the bread has previously been soaked in a litre of milk, but in this case the quantity of other liquids should be reduced accordingly. Sausages prepared with milk, however, spoil more easily.

Wine: Teran

Karst Style Beefsteak

(see picture)

INGREDIENTS:

800 g fillet of beef	
80 g cheese	
80 g prosciutto ham	
8 stoned olives	
30 g mustard	
200 g shallots	
50 g sour cream	
100 g roast meat gravy	
50 ml Teran (Refosco) wine	
pepper	
salt	

Cut the fillet into eight pieces. Beat each piece gently with a meat mallet, add salt and pepper and spread with some mustard. Place a slice of prosciutto ham and some cheese on flour of the steaks, sprinkle with minced olives, then cover with the other four steaks. Briefly fry the steaks in a pan with some hot oil, remove and put in a warm place. Using the oil in which the steaks were cooked, fry the shallots until glassy and add the steak gravy and wine (if Teran wine is unavailable, a rich red Refosco type wine will suffice). Place the beefsteaks into the sauce and braise briefly. Finally, thicken with cream.

Wine: Merlot Barrique — conditioned for several years in an oak cask

Tripe Primorska Style

INGREDIENTS:

1.5 kg tripe	
3 tbsp oil	
50 g bacon	
1 onion	
3 cloves garlic	
a sprig of parsley	
3 tbsp tomato purée	
salt	
pepper	
grated Parmesan cheese	

Wash the tripe thoroughly and cut into strips. Chop the bacon, onion and parsley, and crush the garlic. Heat some oil, add the chopped onion, parsley and bacon. When the onion becomes transparent, add the tripe. Season with salt and pepper and fry for approximately 15 minutes, then add the tomato purée, some water and half the grated Parmesan. Garnish with the remaining Parmesan prior to serving.

Serve with: a light rosé wine or beer

Steak with Figs

INGREDIENTS:

4 beef steaks

50 ml red wine

100 g dark gravy (from steaks)

salt, pepper, mustard

cream (optional)

200 g figs

50 g butter

Beat the steaks, add salt and pepper and spread with mustard. Fry in butter in a pan and then put in a warm place. Pour the red wine and some water into the frying pan (in which the steaks were fried and which now contains the dark gravy) and add salt and pepper, then simmer. Place the steaks back into the pan and add washed slices of figs as well as the cream; allow to boil for a minute.

Serve with sliced potatoes, seasoned with salt and dressed with butter, rosemary and crushed juniper berries, then baked in an oven.

Wine: the same wine as was used in cooking the dish — such as Merlot — is most appropriate

129

Fried Sauerkraut

(see picture)

INGREDIENTS:

1 kg sauerkraut
3 cloves garlic
100 g fat
20 g white flour
4 sausages or the equivalent amount of dried cured pork
a spring of celery
1 onion
1 carrot
a pinch of pepper

Cook the sauerkraut in a little water. Fry some flour in the fat until yellow, add crushed garlic, then add all this to the sauerkraut. Season with pepper. Braise for 15 minutes, occasionally adding water, until it thickens. The sausages or pork should be cooked with the sauerkraut and arranged on the dish before serving.

Budle

INGREDIENTS:

1 kg soft maize flour
10 g salt
100-200 g fatty pork crackling or dried cured bacon
a pinch of pepper
a little white flour

Mix the flour, salt and pepper in a bowl. Melt the fatty crackling or bacon in a frying pan, and add it to the flour, then slowly pour in hot water and stir constantly until a soft dough is formed. Make elongated dumplings from the dough. Sprinkle lightly with white flour, then carefully place into salted boiling water; shaking the pot gently, cook for 10 minutes without stirring. Serve with fried sauerkraut.

Wine: young dry or light dry red wine from the Primorska region

Karst Style Lamb

(see picture)

INGREDIENTS:

a hind quarter of lamb

approx. 50 g butter

pepper

salt

The best meat comes from a six-week-old lamb. The hind parts of the animal, including the legs, are the most suitable. Clean the meat and rub it with salt and pepper. Place in a baking tin, pour the heated butter over it and roast in an oven. Baste the meat continuously to obtain a nice even colour. Make sure that the oven is no too hot and that the meat does not burn.

Serve the lamb with baked potatoes, various salads and vegetable side dishes.

Wine: Barbera from the Primorska region

Brodet

(Fish Soup)

(see picture)

I N G R E D I E N T S:

1 kg assorted fish
1 kg shellfish
150 ml olive oil
1 onion
4–5 cloves garlic
parsley
4 tbsp tomato purée
100 ml white wine
some slices of lemon

Brodet is more savoury if prepared from a variety of fish, and the addition of squid, eels and various shellfish also improves its flavour.

Clean the fish, shellfish and any other sea food, quickly rinse and cut into appropriate-sized pieces. Strain, salt, roll in flour and briefly fry in oil.

Pour some fresh olive oil into a saucepan and fry the thinly sliced onion in it until yellow; then add the chopped garlic and parsley and some tomato purée. Stir well, add the shellfish and some water if necessary.

Allow to boil for approximately 20 minutes then add the fried fish; pour in the white wine, add slices of peeled lemon, salt and pepper. The dish is ready when it comes to the boil. Be careful not to drown the taste of the garlic by adding too much onion.

Serve with *polenta*.

Wine: Malvazija

134

Cod Primorska Style

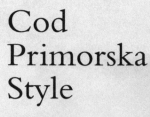

INGREDIENTS:

2 kg cod
4–5 tbsp flour
6–8 cloves garlic
4 tbsp tomato purée
a bay leaf
salt
a few sprigs of parsley
a little grated Parmesan cheese

Clean, scale and fillet the fish thoroughly and carefully remove the skin so that the meat remains intact. Wash and cut into pieces, taking care to remove any remaining bones. Heat some oil in a pan, and fry some flour with chopped garlic. Add the fish, including the skin, and fry for 10 minutes. Stir whilst frying. Add a little water, salt, the bay leaf and tomato purée. Allow to simmer for approximately one hour. Finally, sprinkle with some chopped parsley and Parmesan cheese. Serve with *polenta* or potatoes cooked with the fish.

Wine: Malvazija or Beli Pinot, Chardonnay

Tuna and Tomato Salad

INGREDIENTS:

750 g tomatoes
300 g peppers
100 g peas
200 g tuna in oil
a sprig of basil
Dressing
4 tbsp vinegar
4 tbsp olive oil
salt
pepper

Wash the tomatoes, clean them and cut into slices. Wash and clean the peppers and cut into thin strips. Cook the peas in salted water, strain them and wait to cool. Carefully toss all the ingredients in a bowl, add the tuna, sprinkle with chopped basil and add the dressing. Put the salad into a refrigerator and serve well chilled. Trim with basil leaves.

"Black" Cuttlefish Risotto

(see picture)

INGREDIENTS:

600 g cleaned cuttlefish
300 g rice
1 onion
250 ml white wine
nutmeg flower
2 tbsp tomato purée
olive oil
a little Parmesan cheese
salt

Carefully clean the cuttlefish (taking care not to rupture the ink sacs), then cut into small rings. Chop the onion, fry in olive oil and add the tomato purée and cuttlefish. Add some wine and braise until the cuttlefish softens. Season with salt, pepper and the remaining wine; add rice and some water. Just before the rice is cooked, add the nutmeg and the cuttlefish's ink, stir well so that the ink is evenly distributed, then braise for a short while. Sprinkle with Parmesan before serving.

Wine: the same as that used in preparing the dish — Malvazija or Beli Pinot, Chardonnay

Shark and Rice Salad

INGREDIENTS:

100 g rice
320 g shark
50 g lemon juice
1 onion
2 tomatoes
1 small cucumber
1 sour apple
3 tbsp olive oil
a sprig of basil
dill
chives
salt

Cook the rice gently in salted water in a covered pot; keep it on a low heat for 20 minutes. Clean and wash the shark, remove the skin and cut it into fillets. Sprinkle with a little lemon juice, place on the rice and cook for a further 10 minutes. Remove the cooked fillets and cut them into pieces. Cut the onion into thin slices and, if necessary, peel the cucumber before cutting it into rings; do the same with the tomatoes. Cut the apple into cubes and pour the lemon juice over it.
Put all the ingredients into a bowl, add oil and the remainder of the lemon juice; add the chopped spices and toss carefully. Put the salad into the refrigerator and serve when thoroughly chilled.

Wine: rosé

Fish Rolls with Carrots and Courgettes

(see picture)

INGREDIENTS:

8 fish fillets (e.g. john dory, sea bass or other large sea fish)
4 tbsp lemon juice
250 g carrots
250 g courgettes
800 g butter
salt, pepper
a sprig of parsley
250 ml white wine
250 ml cream

Wash and dry the fish fillets then pour the lemon juice over them and season with salt and pepper.

Clean and wash the carrots and courgettes, cut into long thin strips then blanch in salted water. Mix the butter and chopped parsley and spread it over the fillets. Place the carrots and courgettes over the fillets and roll carefully. Put into a frying pan and fry in olive oil, then add the wine and cream. Braise, then thicken the sauce with a cube of butter kneaded in flour.

Wine: Malvazija or Beli Pinot, Chardonnay

Potato and Spinach Dumplings

(see picture, left side of plate)

INGREDIENTS:

700 g spinach
1 tbsp butter
500 g cooked potatoes
2 egg yolks
100 g white flour
30 g meal (semolina)
basil (to taste)
salt, pepper, nutmeg
Sauce
100 g Gorgonzola and Gauda cheeses
50 g Parmesan cheese
1/2 l vegetable stock and milk
1 tsp cornflour
1 kg tomatoes
2 tbsp olive oil
30 g roasted pine kernels

139

Mash the potatoes and add the braised and chopped spinach, egg yolk, flour and meal. Spice with basil, salt, pepper and freshly grated nutmeg. Mix the ingredients and knead into a dough. Shape dumplings by hand and cook in an uncovered pot in salted water for 12 minutes. In the meantime, prepare the sauce: cut the Gorgonzola into cubes, roughly grate the Gauda and finely grate the Parmesan. Boil the stock and milk, add rosemary and some cornflour; stir in the cheese, which must then melt into the sauce. Peel the tomatoes, remove the seeds and cut into cubes, then braise in olive oil for 3–4 minutes. Add the chopped basil. Sprinkle the roasted pine kernels over the dumplings, and pour the molten cheese over them; finally, dress the dish with the prepared tomatoes.

Bulje

INGREDIENTS:

1 kg maize flour
250 g sugar
250 g butter or margarine
200 g raisins
1 tsp cinnamon

Melt the butter in a pan and pour it together with the flour into a bowl. Add the sugar, raisins and cinnamon, then pour in a little boiling salted water. Mix thoroughly, then shape egg-sized dumpling-like *bulje* from the dough. Carefully place the *bulje* into a pan of boiling water. Cook gently on a low heat for 30 minutes.

Do not stir during cooking, but instead shake the pot several times. The *bulje* are done when they float to the surface.

Serve with sauerkraut or cabbage and dry cured pork.

Wine: rosé

140

Kobarid Štruklji

(see picture)

INGREDIENTS:

Dough

1 kg white flour

400 ml water

salt

Filling

250 g breadcrumbs

250 g butter

250 g walnuts

250 g sugar

250 g raisins

cinnamon, cloves, lemon peel

100 ml white wine or rum

milk

breadcrumbs fried in butter for dressing

Sift the flour, scald with boiling salted water and stir thoroughly with a wooden spoon. When the dough cools, shape it into an elongated roll and cut into pieces. Flatten the pieces by hand into elongated patches. To prepare the filling: fry the breadcrumbs in some butter. Grind the walnuts and add hot salted milk. Clean and wash the raisins thoroughly in warm water, let the water drain off, then add hot wine or soak in rum. Mix all the ingredients together, add cinnamon, ground cloves and chopped lemon peel. The filling must be succulent but, not too moist.

Place some filling on each piece of elongated rolled dough, and mould into walnut-sized pockets by pulling the edge of each *štrukelj* upwards and squeezing the dough, thus sealing the filling inside. Make a small depression in the excess dough on one side of the *štrukelj,* then sprinkle with some flour. Such *štruklji* will keep in the refrigerator for up to two days.

The *štruklji* can be cooked in salted water, fried or grilled. If cooked in water, they must simmer for 30 minutes, but not boil. Rather than stirring whilst cooking, shake the pot several times. When cooked, garnish with fried breadcrumbs. The quantities given yield approximately 50 *štruklji.*

Wine: Sauvignon or Sivi Pinot from the Goriška Brda district

141

Pinca

INGREDIENTS:

500 g flour

40 g yeast

1 egg

100 g sugar

80 g butter

5 egg yolks

lemon peel

a dash of rum

salt

Divide the yeast into three parts. Allow the first part to rise, add the second part and allow to rise, then finally, add the third part together with one egg and allow to rise again. Make a dough from all the ingredients and knead for 30 minutes. Put the dough on buttered paper then, together with the paper, into a cake tin; allow to rise for 3-4 hours. Make an incision in the dough, then bake in an oven.

Gubanica Cake

(see picture)

INGREDIENTS:

Dough

500 g butter

500 g flour

2 eggs

3-4 tbsp white wine

salt

Filling

2 eggs

100 g grated chocolate

100 g almonds

100 g walnuts

100 g pine kernels

candied orange peel

1 tsp citric acid

50 g raisins

100 ml rum

150 g sugar

1 sachet vanilla sugar

a little rum, maraschino liqueur or good white wine

50 g butter

Sift the flour onto a board and divide into two parts. Mix the butter into one part and make a dough. Break the eggs into the second part, add wine and salt, then knead into a separate dough. Separately roll out both parts very thinly — to the thickness of the edge of a knife. Place the butter-dough onto the egg-dough and fold as for puff pastry. Wrap in a wet cloth and allow to rest in a cool place for 3-4 hours. Divide the dough into four parts and make one *gubanica* from each: Roll out each of the four parts, paper-thin. Brush with whisked egg, sprinkle with grated chocolate and a mix of chopped almonds, walnuts, pine kernels, candied orange peel and citric acid. Add the raisins, which should have previously been soaked in rum, and sprinkle with the sugar and vanilla sugar. Sprinkle with rum, maraschino liqueur or white wine and add chunks of butter. Roll the dough into a roulade. Line a cake tin with greaseproof paper, put the rolled cake onto the paper, brush with whisked egg and bake in a moderate oven.

Wine: rich white Primorska wines, Pikolit or Sivi Pinot

Rečca

INGREDIENTS:

250 g butter or unsalted fat or margarine

250 g breadcrumbs

250 g sugar

150 g ground hazelnuts or walnuts

200 g raisins

milk or wine

a sprig of marjoram

rum

1 pig's caul ("rečca")

Fry the marjoram sprig in fat, then add the breadcrumbs and fry until golden brown. Cook the hazelnuts or walnuts in the milk or wine. Thoroughly clean and wash the raisins, strain and then soak in rum. Mix all these ingredients together, then add sugar and mix thoroughly. Stuff the caul with filling, stitch it together and bake in an oven. Cut into slices prior to serving.

Wine: Beli Pinot or Sivi Pinot

143

Index

Page numbers indicated in bold lettering denote an illustration of the dish on the page.

144